M

£6·00

D0412507

COLLEGE OF ARTS AND TECHNOLOGY
LIBRARY

Grammar first 1

Grammar skills
in context
across the curriculum

Ray Barker
Christine Moorcroft

NEWALL GREEN LRC
GREENBROW ROAD
NEWALL GREEN
MANCHESTER M23 2SX
0161 920 4582

Text © Ray Barker and Christine Moorcroft 2002

The right of Ray Barker and Christine Moorcroft to be identified as authors of this work has been asserted by them in accordance with the Copyright, Designs and Patents Act 1988.

All rights reserved. No part of this publication may be reproduced or transmitted in any form or by any means, electronic or mechanical, including photocopy, recording or any information storage and retrieval system, without permission in writing from the publisher or under licence from the Copyright Licensing Agency Limited. Further details of such licences (for reprographic reproduction) may be obtained from the Copyright Licensing Agency Limited, of 90 Tottenham Court Road, London W1P 0LP.

First published in 2002 by:

Nelson Thornes
Delta Place
27 Bath Road
CHELTENHAM GL53 7TH
United Kingdom

02 03 04 05 / 10 9 8 7 6 5 4 3 2 1

A catalogue record for this book is available from the British Library.

ISBN 0-7487-6535-2

Developed and produced by Start to Finish
Typeset by Paul Manning
Printed and bound in China by Wing King Tong

Contents

1 Nouns

In this passage from Macbeth, three witches create an evil mixture by adding ingredients to their cauldron. From this they will cast their spell.

*A **noun** is a word which names a person, place or thing. **Common nouns** name non-specific people, places or things. **Proper nouns** (which always begin with a capital letter) name specific people, places or things.*

First witch: Round about the cauldron go:
 In the poisoned entrails throw;
 Toad, that under cold stone
 Days and nights has thirty one
 Swelter'd venom, sleeping got, 5
 Boil thou first i' the charmed pot.
All: Double, double, toil and trouble;
 Fire burn, and cauldron bubble.
Second witch: Fillet of a fenny snake,
 In the cauldron boil and bake; 10
 Eye of newt, and toe of frog,
 Wool of bat, and tongue of dog;
 Adder's fork, and blind-worm's sting,
 Lizard's leg, and howlet's wing;
 For a charm of powerful trouble, 15
 Like a hell-broth boil and bubble.
All: Double, double, toil and trouble;
 Fire burn, and cauldron bubble.
Third witch: Scale of dragon, tooth of wolf,
 Witch's mummy, maw and gulf 20
 Of the ravin'd salt-sea shark;
 Root of hemlock, digg'd i' the dark;
 Liver of blaspheming Jew,
 Gall of goat, and slips of yew
 Slivered in the moon's eclipse; 25
 Nose of Turk, and Tartar's lips;
 Finger of birth-strangled babe,
 Ditch-delivered by a drab,
 Make the gruel thick and slab:
 Add thereto a tiger's chaudron, 30
 For the ingredients of our cauldron.
All: Double, double, toil and trouble;
 Fire burn, and cauldron bubble.

from Macbeth
by William Shakespeare
(genre: classic drama)

Glossary

chaudron entrails
drab prostitute
fenny living in a marsh
gulf stomach
howlet a young owl
ravin'd finished devouring its prey
swelter'd sweated
witch's mummy mummified part of a witch

Read on!

1 When you read this passage, what do you notice about the layout of the writing and the sounds you create?

2 How does the list of 'things' make you feel? Why?

3 Identify the nouns in the passage. Copy and complete the chart. Which type of noun is most used?

People	Places	Things

Write on!

1 Some nouns simply state what a thing is. Some nouns create emotional impact. Complete a chart like this:

Noun	Feeling
stone	none
entrails	messy, bloody, nasty

2 Create your own list of 'nasty nouns' to write your own spell to make your school disappear. Write the spell. It need not rhyme, but should concentrate on the rhythm and could end in the 'Double, double …' lines from Shakespeare.

3 Identify any proper nouns in the passage and explain why this category of noun begins with a capital letter.

Over to you!

1 Nouns sometimes have short words such as *the*, *a* or *an* before them. These words are called **articles**. Find examples in the passage and the nouns to which they refer.

Article	Noun	Article	Noun
a		the	

2 Articles are tiny words but they are often essential to make sense. The Activity Sheet will help you to prove this. When is *an* used rather than *a*? What happens with words such as *hotel*, and why?

3 Explain the difference in meaning between the following:
a) I want the chocolate in the box.
   I want a chocolate in the box.
b) The dog has escaped.
   A dog has escaped
c) She has taken the umbrella.
   She has taken an umbrella.

2 Verbs

In this poem Robert Southey describes a fast-flowing river.
   Verbs *are words, or groups of words, which indicate an action or a state of being. They tell you what someone or something is doing or being. Sentences must contain a verb.*

The cataract strong then plunges along;
Striking and raging as if war waging
Its caverns and rocks among:
Rising and leaping, sinking and creeping,
Swelling and sweeping, showering and springing,   5
Plying and flinging, writhing and wringing,
Eddying and whisking, spouting and frisking,
Turning and twisting, around and around
With endless rebound …

And threading and spreading and whizzing and hissing   10
And dripping and skipping and hitting and splitting,
And shining and twining and rattling and battling,
And shaking and quaking, and pouring and roaring,
And waving and raving, and tossing and crossing,
And flowing and going, and running and stunning,   15
And foaming and roaming, and dinning and spinning,
And dropping and hopping, and working and jerking,
And guggling and struggling, and heaving and cleaving
And moaning and groaning;
And glittering and frittering, and gathering and feathering,   20
And whitening and brightening, and quivering and shivering,
And flurrying and scurrying, and thundering and floundering …

Recoiling, turmoiling and toiling and boiling,
And gleaming and streaming and steaming and beaming,
And rushing and flushing and brushing and gushing,   25
And flapping and rapping and clapping and slapping,
And curling and whirling and purling and twirling,
And thumping and plumping and bumping and jumping,
And dashing and flashing and splashing and clashing.

from 'The Cataract of Lodore'
by Robert Southey
(genre: classic poetry)

Glossary
cataract a fast-flowing river

Read on!

1 What do you notice immediately about the words chosen by this writer to achieve his effect?

2 How does his use of this particular tense of the verb help him to achieve the effect of a fast-flowing river?

3 How do you know which words are verbs? Test this out with *strong* and *plunges* in the first line. Write the 'verb' in full. Decide which parts of the verb may have to change. The Activity Sheet will help.

4 Identify all the verbs in the passage. Write out the original verb form.

Verb in passage	Original verb form
striking	to strike

Write on!

1 Write the verbs from the first verse in complete sentences. Underline the verbs.

The river is striking and raging among the caverns and rocks. It is rising and leaping.

2 Re-write the passage, changing the tense of the verb.

Present tense: *The river strikes and rages among the caverns ...*

Past tense: *The river struck and raged among the caverns ...*

3 Discuss what difference the change of tense makes to meaning and effect: for example, many of the verbs in the original passage are in the **continuous present tense** (using the -ing endings), suggesting that the movements are happening now. What happens when the verb changes?

Over to you!

1 Write your own passage, using the continuous present tense, about the waves of the sea in a storm or a crowd of people at a sports event or pop concert. It does not have to be in verse, but use the verbs to create movement and excitement.
   • Try to create effects with the verbs: rhyme them or make the sounds clash.
   • Use onomatopoeic verbs.
   • Use a thesaurus to find a selection of verbs with similar meanings.
   • Decide which tense or form of the verb will achieve your effect.
   • To create a feeling of speed and breathlessness, do you need short or long sentences? How many times do you need to use *and*?

Walk	Run
to stumble	to gallop
Speak	**Sounds**
to scream	to rumble

2 How would a geography textbook describe the fast-flowing river? Make a list of verbs it would use, and the appropriate tense, and comment on the style it is trying to achieve.

3 Write the account and compare it to others in this section under the headings of: Purpose, Effects, Audience, Stylistic features.

3 Adjectives

The author describes two characters, making the adjectives he uses show how he feels about the two men.

Adjectives *are words which describe nouns or pronouns.*

Johnny Sharp wore a grey homburg hat, rather on the back of his head and cocked sideways, with the brim turned down in front. He had a foxy sort of face – narrow eyes, long thin nose, long thin lips; he grinned a lot, showing his bad teeth and a gold-stopped one on the left of his upper jaw. He had a loud check suit with padded shoulders, and a perfectly ghastly tie with large patterns on it like drawing room curtains. He had two flashy rings on his right hand, and a habit of flopping this hand at you while he was talking. He was a narrow, wriggling sort of chap, from top to bottom; like a dressed-up eel. Or a snake.

The Wart … had a round, pasty face, and eyes that slithered about when he spoke to people. He never wore a hat. His hair was Brylcreemed, bunchy at the back. He generally wore a bluish tweed sports coat, with two slits behind, and dirty, fawn-coloured flannel trousers very broad at the bottom and trailing over his down-at-heel shoes. Everything about him looked rather scruffy. His real name was Joseph Seeds, but everyone called him the Wart because he had a huge wart on his right cheek with whiskers growing out of it. And because he was a wart.

from The Otterbury Incident
by C. Day-Lewis
(genre: children's fiction)

Read on!

1 Choose five objects from your surroundings. Copy and complete this chart to show the variety of adjectives you can use in description.

Object	Shape	Size	Colour	Texture
desk	rectangular	large	brown	smooth

2 These are 'factual' adjectives; they do not show how you feel about the objects. Write 'factual' sentences about these objects. Then choose adjectives which show emotion and write about your five objects in sentences, for example:

The rectangular, brown desk stood in the corner of the classroom.

The ugly rectangular, brown desk stood in the corner of the classroom.

3 Discuss the differences between these sentences, showing the effect of your choice of adjectives.
4 Look closely at the description of Johnny Sharp. List the adjectives the author uses.
5 Decide which of these are 'factual' and which of them reveal the author's attitude towards the character. If any attitude is revealed, explain how the author feels and how this is communicated to you. The chart may help.

'Factual' adjectives	Adjectives showing attitude	Attitude revealed	How I know this

Write on!

1 Continue with each description for a few sentences, choosing adjectives which create the same impression.
2 Write the description of Johnny Sharp as if it were completely factual. Remove all the emotional effect of the adjectives. Is this kind of description suitable for a novel?
3 Re-write the description of the Wart to make his character more favourable. Which adjectives will you use to do this? The Activity Sheet will help.

Over to you!

1 Imagine that one of your classmates is missing. The police interview you and ask for a description. What kind of description would they want? What use would they make of such a description? How accurate does it have to be? List the features you would describe and the adjectives you would use to describe them.

DESCRIPTION
Height: 1 m 50 cm
Hair: light brown
Eyes: blue
Nose: thin and long

2 Re-write this description for a character in a novel. The list of features will be useful, but the audience and the purpose of the writing have changed. How will your choice of adjectives have to change to reflect this? You can now express like or dislike – an emotional response to the character.

DESCRIPTION
Her light brown hair was greasy and hung limply around her shoulders.
His cold blue eyes stared at me, without pity.

4 Adverbs

Annie has been hired to teach Helen Keller – a deaf, dumb and blind child. In this passage she is convincing Helen's family that she will have to be tough.

Adverbs *add information to verbs. They tell us how, when or where something happens.*

Annie: She's testing you. You realise?

James: *(to Annie)* She's testing you.

Keller: Jimmie be quiet. *(James sits tensely)* Now she's home, naturally she –

Annie: And wants to see what will happen. At your hands. I said it was my main worry, is this what you promised me not half an hour ago?

Keller: *(reasonably)* But she's *not* kicking now –

Annie: *(patiently)* And not learning not to. Mrs Keller, teaching her is bound to be painful, to everyone. I know it hurts to watch, but she'll live up to just what you demand of her and no more.

James: *(palely)* She's testing *you.*

Keller: *(testily)* Jimmie.

James: I have an opinion, I think I should –

Keller: No one's interested in hearing your opinion.

Annie: *I'm* interested, of course she's testing me. Let me keep her to what she's learned and she'll go on learning from me. Take her out of my hands and it all comes apart. *(Kate closes her eyes, digesting it; Annie sits again, with a brief comment for her.) Be* bountiful, it's at her expense. *(She turns to James, flatly.)* Please pass me more of her favourite foods.

(Then Kate lifts Helen's hand, and turning her towards Annie, surrenders her; Helen makes for her own chair.)

Kate: *(low)* Take her, Miss Annie.

Annie: Thank you.

from The Miracle Worker
by William Gibson
(genre: drama)

Read on!

1 Identify the adverbs in the playscript. Adverbs describe verbs. Complete the chart to show what actions they describe, even if the verb is not present, as here.

Adverb	Action it describes
tensely	sits (verb: to sit)

2 What suffix do all these adverbs use? Is it true to say that all adverbs end in this suffix?

3 Explain what is added to the description by the use of each of these adverbs in the playscript.

He sits.
He sits tensely.

You may need to use a dictionary: for example, *tensely* suggests that the character is holding himself nervously because he is not sure of the situation.

Write on!

1 Adverbs tell us **how**, **when** and **where**. These three characteristics are called **manner**, **time** and **place**. Complete a chart with suitable adverbs to match ten verbs you have chosen. Which adverbs mainly end with the suffix *-ly*? The Activity Sheet will help.

2 Use some of these ten examples to continue the playscript. Use adverbs to give the actors as much help as you can to interpret the characters.

Over to you!

1 Adverbs are often used to add information to vague verbs. Write a simple sentence: for instance, *'I want to go to the club,'* she said. List ten adverbs which will describe the different ways she said the words and explain the difference each word makes to how the audience feels.

'I want to go to the club,' she said pleadingly.	*Makes us feel sorry for her. She is asking for help.*
'*I want to go to the club,*' she said defiantly.	*She becomes more aggressive. Sounds determined.*

2 List verbs which could explain the same situation: for instance, *she said quietly* could mean the same as *she whispered*.

3 Create a list of ten adverbs and transform them into other parts of speech, where possible, to ensure that you understand the difference between adverbs, adjectives and nouns.

Adverb	Adjective	Noun
beautifully	beautiful	beauty

5 Prepositions

In this poem, John Clare describes a scene in the countryside.
Prepositions *tell you how one thing is related to another – the position of things or people in relation to another part of the sentence.*

The rustling of leaves under the feet in woods and under hedges;
The crumbling of cat-ice and snow down wood rides, narrow lanes
    and every street causeway;
Rustling through a wood or rather rushing, while the wind haloos
    in the oak-top like thunder;   5
The rustle of birds' wings startled from their nests or flying unseen
    into the bushes;
The whizzing of larger birds overhead in the wood, such as crows,
    puddocks, buzzards;
The trample of robins and woodlarks on the brown leaves, and the   10
    patter of squirrels on the green moss;
The fall of an acorn on the ground, the pattering of nuts on the hazel
    branches as they fall from ripeness;
The flirt of the groundlark's wing from the stubble – how sweet such
    pictures on dewy mornings, when the dew flashes from its brown feathers!   15

from 'Pleasant sounds'
by John Clare (genre: classic poetry)

Glossary

cat-ice a slang phrase for thin ice
flirt a light movement
haloos calls loudly
puddock a bird

Read on!

1. The poem is about the 'pictures' conjured up by the countryside in the mind of this nineteenth-century poet. Write what he notices in each line.
2. Which sense does the poet most use in communicating these pictures? Write your evidence in a chart:

Touch	
Taste	
Hearing	rustling of leaves
Smell	
Sight	

3. Identify the prepositions in the poem. Remember that prepositions show the position or relationship between nouns or pronouns. Without this relationship, the sentence is nonsense. Use a chart to show this relationship.

Noun or pronoun	Preposition – shows relationship	Noun or pronoun
leaves	under	feet

Write on!

1. Prepositions are to do either with **place** or **time**. Find ten more prepositions to complete a chart like this.

Place	Time
1 under a tree	1 away since yesterday
2	2

2. Write sentences or a paragraph using some of the examples you have found.
3. Change some of the prepositions in the poem. What different effects are produced? For instance, what is the difference in meaning between a bird startled from its nest and a bird startled on its nest? Look at the chart above to examine the function the word is performing in the sentence.
4. Re-write the poem with different prepositions of your choice to create a completely different atmosphere. It could be a supernatural or fantasy effect: for instance, the rustling of leaves **in** the feet. Read this when you have finished and note how important your choice of such small words can be.

Over to you!

1. Write directions for a visitor to your school. Try doing this without using prepositions. Is it possible? Complete the directions using prepositions.

   Walk ... the road. Take the first left ... the bridge.

2. Draw a simple mathematical diagram consisting of geometrical shapes – circles, squares, triangles. Describe it to a partner using appropriate language so that he or she can draw it. The Activity Sheet will help.
   - Which prepositions are the most useful in such descriptions?

6 Pronouns

In this passage William Golding writes about a character fighting for his life in the sea.

Pronouns *are used instead of nouns to avoid repeating nouns in your writing.*

Immediately he was convulsed and struggling. His legs kicked and swung sideways. His head ground against rock and turned. He scrabbled in the white water with both hands and heaved himself up. He felt the too-smooth wetness running on his face and the brilliant jab of pain at the corner of his right eye. He spat and snarled. He glimpsed the trenches with their thick layers of dirty white, their trapped inches of solution, a gull slipping away over a green sea. Then he was forcing himself forward. He fell into the next trench, hauled himself over the wall, saw a jumble of broken rock, slid and stumbled. He was going down hill and he fell part of the way. There was moving water round flattish rocks, a complication of weedy life. The wind went down with him and urged him forward. As long as he went forward the wind was satisfied, but if he stopped for a moment's caution it thrust his unbalanced body down so that he scraped and hit. He saw little of the open sea and sky or the whole rock but only flashes of intimate being, a crack or point, a hand's breath of yellowish surface that was about to strike a blow, unavoidable fists of rock that beat him impersonally, struck bright flashes of light from his body. The pain in the corner of his eye went with him too. This was the most important of all the pains because it thrust a needle now into the dark skull where he lived. The pain could not be avoided. His body revolved around it. Then he was holding brown weed and the sea was washing over his head and shoulders. He pulled himself up and lay on a flat rock with a pool across the top.

from Pincher Martin
by William Golding
(genre: fiction)

Read on!

1   This novel is about one person, whose name is the title. What do you notice about the way the author refers to this character throughout the passage?

2   Which pronouns are used to represent the character in this passage? Why do you think the author has done this?

3   'Pronoun' means 'for a noun'. Which nouns could replace the pronouns used in this passage? To whom or to what do the pronouns refer?

4   There are various kinds of pronouns. From the definitions given below, decide which of the limited range used in the passage are personal pronouns and which are possessive pronouns.

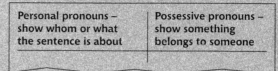

Personal pronouns – show whom or what the sentence is about	Possessive pronouns – show something belongs to someone

Write on!

1   Re-write the first five sentences of the passage replacing all the pronouns with the correct name of the character. What effect does this create?

   Immediately Pincher Martin was convulsed and struggling. Pincher Martin's legs kicked …

2   Edit your work to balance the use of nouns and the use of pronouns for maximum effect.

3   Re-write the entire passage so that it contains a variety of nouns and pronouns. The Activity Sheet will help.
   • Be careful to avoid repetition of names; this could be boring.
   • Avoid creating ambiguity – more than one meaning – by using *he* and *him* unclearly.

4   When you have finished, discuss whether you think your version, using a variety of nouns and pronouns, is better than Golding's original.
   • Has making the character more personal by naming him changed the effect of mystery?
   • Has this taken away from the idea of struggle, which is what makes the passage so moving?
   • Does it become just an account rather than an emotional experience?
   • Is it clearer what is happening?

Over to you!

The passage deals with the singular – just one person is described, Pincher Martin. Re-write the passage as if it were about a group of people struggling in the sea. Use pronouns in the plural. You may have to change other words to make sense.

Immediately they were convulsed …

Plural personal pronouns (as the subject of the verb)	Plural personal pronouns (as the object of the verb)	Plural possessive pronouns
we, you, they	us, you, them	our, your, their,

7 Making your meaning clear

Archy is a cockroach living in New York with Mehitabel the alley cat. He is really the reincarnated spirit of a poet and still likes to write poetry. His problem is that he has to fling himself at a typewriter to hit the keys and cannot hold down the shift key to deal with punctuation and upper case letters.

The comic poetry he produces is therefore without grammatically correct phrasing and punctuation, but is still both witty and philosophical.

the flattered lightning bug

a lightning bug got
in here the other night a
regular hick from
the real country he was
awful proud of himself you   5
city insects may think
you are some punkins
but i don t see any
of you flashing in the dark
like we do in   10
the country all right go
to it says i mehitabel the
cat and that green
spider who lives in your locker
and two or three cockroach   15
friends of mine and a
friendly rat all gathered

around him and urged him on
and he lightened you
don t see anything like this   20
in town often he says go to it
we told him it s a
real treat to us and
we nicknamed him broadway
which pleased him   25
this is the life
he said all i
need is a harbour
under me to be a
statue of liberty and   30
he got so vain of
himself i had to take
him down a peg you ve
made lightning for two hours
little bug i told him   35
but i don t hear
any claps of thunder
yet there are some men
like that when he wore
himself out mehitabel   40
the cat ate him

archy

from archy and mehitabel
by Don Marquis

Glossary

a lightning bug a fire fly
punkins slang term for 'the best'

Read on!

1 What do you notice about the passage immediately you start reading?
2 Explain the joke in the poem about why Archy would write in this way.
3 What ideas can you understand? List them.
4 How much context do you need to make the meaning clear?
5 What do you know about the words which can start a sentence and those which cannot? *He* and *she* can start sentences, whereas *and* usually does not.

6 Which of the following make this passage difficult to understand? Copy and complete the chart.

Difficulty?	Yes/No	Why?
No capitals at the beginning of sentences		
No full stops		
No paragraphs		
No context		
No other punctuation		

Write on!

1 Use the Activity Sheet to mark where you think the full stops should go in this passage. Compare your version with a partner's.
   - Is there any disagreement about where the sentences begin and end?
   - Is it possible to have punctuation in different places and still make sense?
   - Does it make the same sense?
   - Is the meaning different?

2 Continue with the same technique for ten more lines of the poem. Give this to a partner to punctuate correctly.
   - Discuss the way in which the person's punctuation has improved or altered the meaning of your original.
   - Which is the better style to communicate the situation in which Archy finds himself?
   - How much context is needed for someone to be able to understand your work?

Over to you!

1 Write the same story as a simple report using the past tense:
   Archy said that a lightning bug ...
   Report the speech. What different kinds of punctuation are you using from the original to write in this genre?
2 Re-write the passage so that it contains complete sentences which give more information.
   Last night a lightning bug got in here to talk to us. He was a regular hick from the real country ...

   - Discuss the effect which this has on the tone of the passage and on the character who is created by speaking the words.
   - Compare your paragraphing with the demarcation of lines in the poem. Can you find any sense behind the poet's choices?
   - What extra words do you use to make connections between the sentences?

8 Commas

In this autobiographical poem, Walt Whitman describes Manhattan (New York) in the early nineteenth century.

__Commas__ separate words, phrases and clauses. They stand for a short pause and are not as strong as full stops. In this passage commas are mainly used to separate items in a list.

Manhattan … superb, with tall and wonderful spires,
Rich, hemmed thick all round with sailships and steamships – an island sixteen
    miles long, solid-founded,
Numberless crowded streets – high growths of iron, slender, strong, light,
    splendidly uprising toward clear skies;
Tide swift and ample, well-loved by me, toward sun-down,
The flowing sea-currents, the little islands, larger adjoining islands, the heights, the
    villas,   5
The countless masts, the white shore-steamers, the lighters, the ferry-boats, the
    black sea-steamers well modelled;
The down-town streets, the jobbers' houses of business – the business of the ship-
    merchants, the money-brokers – the river streets;
Immigrants arriving, fifteen to twenty thousand a week;
The carts hauling goods – the manly race of drivers of horses – the brown-faced
    sailors;
The summer air, the bright sun shining, and the sailing clouds aloft;   10
The winter snows, the sleigh-bells – the broken ice in the river, passing along, up or
    down, with the flood-tide or the ebb-tide;
The mechanics of the city, the masters, well-formed, beautiful-faced, looking you
    straight in the eyes;
The parades, processions, bugles playing, flags flying, drums beating;
A million people – manners free and superb – open voices – hospitality –the most
    courageous and friendly young men;
The free city! No slaves! No owners of slaves!   15
The beautiful city, the city of hurries and sparkling waters! The city of spires and
    masts!
The city nested in bays! My city!

from 'Leaves of Grass'
by Walt Whitman
(genre: classic American poetry)

Read on!

1 How can you tell that the author is excited by what he sees? Find examples of:
   a) exclamations
   b) short, breathy, incomplete sentences
   c) dashes to add information as he remembers it
   d) repetition of sentence structures.
2 What does he find most impressive about this growing city?
3 How does he communicate to you all the wonderful things to be found in the city?
4 Why do you think he relies so much on lists in the poem? What effect does he create by using them so much?

5 When you list words in a sentence you need to separate the individual components, or the sentence will not make any sense. For example, in line 3, 'high growths of iron slender strong light splendidly uprising toward clear skies', without commas we can understand the first words – 'high growths of iron' – but what is a 'slender strong light'? All the items are considered as one.

Use the Activity Sheet to decide where commas can most effectively be placed to make the writer's meaning clear.

Write on!

1 In line 1, the comma is used to present a short pause in the sense. Re-write this line as complete sentences: for instance, *Manhattan is superb. It has …*
2 Find two other examples of where commas are used like this in the poem. Re-write the lines and discuss the different effect which is achieved by omitting the commas.
3 Commas are also used at the end of the lines of poetry, to break the verse and, more importantly, to ensure that there are no short sentences. This communicates a sense of the writer's excitement as he rushes forward, telling you everything about the city he loves. Re-write the first ten lines so that they end in full stops. You will have to add some words. Discuss the different effect which is achieved without the commas.
4 Take five of the lists and re-write them without commas. You will need to make the sentences much longer: for example, *There are numberless crowded streets with high growths of iron. These are slender and strong. They are also light as they rise splendidly to the skies.* Discuss the different effect which is achieved without the commas.

Over to you!

Write a similar account of the place where you live or would like to live. List everything you like about it and communicate some of your excitement using lists, appropriately punctuated with commas. Use the same structure as the poem if it helps. You do not need to write a poem but, if you do, it can be in free verse like the original.

London … superb, with tall and towering skyscrapers.
Rich …

9 Semi-colons

Herman Melville describes the hunting of a white whale (Moby Dick).
Semi-colons *are used instead of full stops to separate two closely-linked main clauses of similar importance or to break up long and complicated items in a list.*

It was a sight full of quick wonder and awe! The vast swell of the omnipotent sea; the surging, hollow roar they made, as they rolled along the eight gunwales, like gigantic bowls in a boundless bowling green; the brief suspected agony of the boat, as it would tip for an instant on the knife-like edge of the sharper waves, that almost seemed threatening to cut it in two; the sudden profound dip into the watery glens and hollows; the keen spurrings and goadings to gain the top of the opposite hill; the headlong, sled-like slides down its other side; all these, with the cries of the headsmen and the harpooners, and the shuddering gasps of the oarsmen, with the wondrous sight of the ivory *Pequod* bearing down upon her boats with outstretched sails, like a wild hen after her screaming brood; all this was thrilling. Not the raw recruit marching from the bosom of his wife into the fever heat of his first battle; not the dead man's ghost encountering the first unknown phantom in the other world; neither of these can feel stranger and stronger emotions than that man does, who for the first time finds himself pulling into the charmed, churned circle of the sperm-whale.

from Moby Dick *by Herman Melville
(genre: classic novel)*

Glossary

gunwale the upper edge of the ship's side
omnipotent all-powerful
spurrings and goadings ways of driving people forward

Read on!

1 Identify the semi-colons used in the passage.
2 From which two punctuation marks is a semi-colon made? How does this help you to understand how the semi-colon works as a punctuation mark?
3 How does the author communicate his excitement to the reader?
4 What do you notice about the length of the sentences Melville uses? Why do you think he chose this stylistic feature for his subject matter?
5 What are some of the problems faced when writing such sentences? How can a writer overcome these?

Write on!

1 Re-write the second sentence, making it into a series of much shorter sentences by using full stops.
   - What effect is produced? Are the sentences too short and 'jerky'?
   - Is this version as effective as the original in expressing the excitement of the chase? Give your reasons.
2 Re-write the second sentence, making it into a series of shorter sentences by using full stops and connectives such as *and*, *but* and *however*, instead of the semi-colons.
   - What effect is produced? Is it dramatic enough?
   - Is this version as effective as the original? Give your reasons.
3 Re-write the second sentence, using commas instead of semi-colons.
   - Does this version make sense?
   - What effect is produced?
   - Is the use of commas appropriate for this kind of list?
   - Is this version as effective as the original? Give your reasons.

Over to you!

1 Re-write the last sentence as two or three separate sentences, using full stops and connectives, and changing words appropriately. Discuss the effect you have produced and, if it as good as the original, say why. The Activity Sheet will help.
2 Write a paragraph about an exciting chase or race in which you have been involved.
   - Use long sentences and semi-colons in the first part to carry the audience along in a breathless rush of events.
   - Show how semi-colons rather than full stops can create drama through short dramatic statements.
   - In the second part, list the reasons why the experience was exciting. Use semi-colons instead of commas to divide the parts of this list.

10 Apostrophes

*This is a fictional diary which includes information about issues connected with health. It contains **apostrophes** used for two purposes: to show possession and to indicate missing letters in a contraction.*

Wednesday 11th January

The biology teacher set me off today. Going on and on about how wonderful and efficient our heart is, giving 80 beats per minute, which makes 3 billion pumps during a whole lifetime. Estimated mine's already done 80 times 60 times 24 times 365 times 14 = 588,672,000 beats. (My calculator ran out of space – need a better one.) Worried about all this work my heart's already done; felt sure it would never last out. Asked Mrs Smellie whether I was likely to have a heart attack in the afternoon's cross-country run. After all, Grandad died of a heart attack dashing for a bus last year. Know he was 80 but was dead worried it might run in the family. Smellie said not to be stupid. Exercise is good for the heart and helps stop heart attacks when we're older – just like NOT smoking does. She never misses a chance of telling us how wonderful NOT smoking is. Said the odds of me dying from a heart attack at my age are less than one in a million anyway – less likely than winning the National Lottery. Next worry was Mrs Smellie remarking that I was actually suffering from a bad attack of 'hypochondriasis'. Sounds much worse – suppose I die of it? Asked what the symptoms were, but got nowhere. She just told me to 'look it up'. Might just get around to it, if I don't die tonight.

Thursday 12th January

Still alive. Managed a second day of my diary! New Year's resolution was to start on 1st January – only 10 days late! It was reading *Adrian Mole* and my mum stopping nagging that inspired me.

Nothing much happened today except my sister, Susie, kept on at Mum about having Kate as well as Mary for her 13th birthday party. I hate them all – they're so boring. Mary's the sixth 'best friend' she's had in a week. Mum's taking them to some dismal Walt Disney film on Monday for the fourth time. Really babyish but it's the only thing on. I'm going to go to Sam's instead.

Haven't died from hypochondriasis disease yet – perhaps it's not as serious as I thought. Sam's dad will know – he's an expert.

Sunday 15th January

Forced up by Mum at 12 o'clock.

Thursday 17th January

GREAT DAY. Got to school early. Amazed everybody including myself. Arrived just as Whitton, the caretaker, was opening up. Very surprised to see ME at that time, normally catches me sneaking in behind the bicycle sheds after the bell's gone. I usually find myself tripping over a crowd of sixth-formers all smoking. Told Whitton I'd some work to do in the library. Took down the dictionary with clammy palms – and here we were. 'HYDROPHOBIA – an aversion to water, especially as a symptom of rabies.' Help, this was something else I had got as I hate baths. 'HYPNOSIS – state like sleep in which subject acts only on external suggestion.' I began to wonder whether I had everything in the dictionary. 'HYPOCHONDRIASIS – abnormal anxiety about one's health.' So that's all it is. I'm a person who has an abnormal anxiety about his health and not a terrible disease.

From The New Diary
of a Teenage Health Freak
by Aidan MacFarlane and Ann McPherson
(genre: diary)

Read on!

1 Make a chart on which to list the apostrophes in the passage. Notice the purpose of each apostrophe:

Contractions: apostrophes to show missing letters	What is the complete version?	Apostrophes to show possession	What belongs to whom (or what)?

2 a) Re-write in full (with no contractions) the sentences from the passage in which there are apostrophes showing a contraction.

The sentences must still have the same meaning.

b) What difference does this make to the style of the passage?

c) Why do you think the author used contractions?

3 How can possession be shown without the use of apostrophes?

4 a) Alter and re-write the sentences in which there are apostrophes showing possession, but without the apostrophes.

The sentences must still show the same possession but in a different way.

b) What difference does this make to the style of the passage?

Write on!

1 Re-write the following text in the style of the passage:

Use apostrophes

I lost my bike, so I rode the one belonging to Sam. It is a full-size one and the seat of it is a lot higher than I would have liked. As I am fairly short I could not handle it and, suddenly, I could not find the brakes I slid on some ice. As I flew over the handlebars I heard something CRACK. The next thing I remember was being in the ambulance. The faces of the paramedics were the first things I saw. I could not understand what had happened.

The doctor showed me the x-ray and said I was lucky not to have damaged my brain. She said she could not understand why people did not wear crash helmets when cycling because 200 cyclists are killed and 24,000 injured in England and Wales each year. It does not even seem safe to walk around, as 1,300 pedestrians are killed and 49,000 injured each year. All this does not even include other types of accidents, like drowning.

Because I had been knocked out they said I might have to stay in hospital overnight. I was looking forward to the visits of my friends.

2 Write rules for using apostrophes:
* with both singular and plural nouns to show possession
* in contractions
* in omissions
* in the word *its*.

Over to you!

Write your own diary entry about a health issue. Use an informal style similar to that of the passage, and include contractions and possessives. The Activity Sheet will help.

11 Dashes and brackets

In this passage from his autobiography, Michael Heseltine describes an incident during his schooldays.

*The author uses **dashes** and **brackets** to surround parts of sentences which add extra information.*

Broughton was a happy place, a successful school with a firm but respected headmaster. Curiously, there was another side to it of which I was virtually unaware until I received an invitation in late 1946 to appear in court in defence of my headmaster. Another school, Brockhurst from Newbury in Berkshire, owned by one John Fergus Park, had been boarded on us for a couple of years. We apparently had the space and it was commonplace in wartime for schools (particularly evacuated ones) to share premises. But in this case the two headmasters did not get on. Although I have no memory of the Brockhurst boys ever being set against the Broughton boys, Julian Critchley [writer, broadcaster, journalist and Conservative Member of Parliament] claims that they were. Julian was two years older than me and was the elder son of Dr MacDonald

Critchley, the leading neurologist. By coincidence, our lives were to cross and re-cross many times – at prep school, public school, Oxford, in publishing and finally as Members of Parliament.

Certainly the whole saga ended dramatically enough. It culminated in a civil action just before my fourteenth birthday. By then I had left Broughton to go to Shrewsbury. Three of my former schoolmates and I were invited to appear in the witness box first to be examined by a counsel for our old headmaster, Mr Thompson (who was claiming damages for trespass and assault), and then to be cross-examined by Mr Park, who was conducting his own case.

In an earnest croak – my voice was just about to break – I related how Brockhurst boys had shouted 'things' at Broughton boys, and that I had written to my parents to tell them that there was a rumour that Mr Park had bought Broughton and saying, 'If you don't mind, I want to leave immediately.' The questioning seemed extraordinarily banal. At one stage Mr Park asked whether I had ever climbed trees at school, to which I replied, 'Yes, often – on the sly.' At this point Mr Justice Wrottesley intervened to ask, 'Did you ever get whacked for it?' 'I never got caught, my Lord,' was my answer to that. It was not exactly F.E. Smith-style [a lawyer who wrote *Famous Trials*] repartee, but it still seemed to amuse the court.

from Life in the Jungle: My Autobiography,
by Michael Heseltine
(genre: autobiography)

Read on!

1 In the passage find sections of sentences which have been separated by round or square brackets or by dashes.
   a) Copy those sentences and mask the separated parts.
   b) Read the part which remains. Is it still a sentence? Explain how you can tell.
2 a) Would it matter, grammatically, if those parts were left out?
   b) Would it matter for the sense of the passage if they were left out?
3 Explain the purposes for which the author uses round brackets and dashes.

4 Give an example of a sentence in which commas have been used for a similar purpose.

> *To check your answer, write out the sentences, omitting the part surrounded by the commas; read what is left of each sentence and check that it still makes sense.*

5 The words enclosed by square brackets have been added for the purposes of this book. Explain how they help the reader, and why they have been enclosed in square brackets.

Write on!

1 a) Read the following sentences. Re-write them as one sentence, using dashes, brackets, or both, to combine them:
      i) I wanted to be a singer.
      ii) I had always sung reggae music with my father.
      iii) He used to sing in a local band in Jamaica.
      iv) So I joined a band in Notting Hill.
   b) What information do you need to add for readers who do not know what reggae music is? Write a sentence.
   c) Underline the most important words in the sentence you have written. Use square brackets to add them to sentence (ii).
2 a) Read the following sentences. Re-write them as one sentence, using dashes, brackets, or both, to combine them:
      i) I went to Halewood Village school.
      ii) It was a happy school.
      iii) It must have been built by the 1880s because my great-grandfather went there.
      iv) He left at the age of twelve to work on the family's farm.
   b) How can you tell readers who do not know that Halewood is a suburb of Liverpool, without interrupting the flow of your narrative? Write a sentence.
   c) Underline the most important words in the sentence you have written. Use square brackets to add them to sentence (i).

Over to you!

1 Make notes about events from your past.
2 Write the outline for a recount of the events. The Activity Sheet will help.
3 Add information to make the recount more interesting or to give information (for example, about anything which might be unfamiliar to the reader).
4 Redraft the recount. Separate extra information from the rest of the sentences with brackets or dashes.

12 Sentences and style

Charles Dickens describes a rather boastful character. He carefully crafts his sentences not only to make the physical description vivid, but also to give the reader a sense of the person's character.

Why, Mr Bounderby was as near Mr Gradgrind's bosom friend, as a man perfectly devoid of sentiment can approach that spiritual relationship towards another man perfectly devoid of sentiment. So near was Mr Bounderby – or, if the reader should prefer it, so far off.

He was a rich man; banker, merchant, manufacturer, and what not. A big, loud man, with a stare and a metallic laugh. A man made out of a coarse material, which seemed to have been stretched to make much of him. A man with a great puffed head and forehead, swelled veins in his temples, and such a strained skin to his face that it seemed to hold his eyes open and lift his eyebrows up. A man with a pervading appearance on him of being inflated like a balloon, and ready to start. A man who could never sufficiently vaunt himself a self-made man. A man who was always proclaiming, through his brassy speaking trumpet of a voice of his, his old ignorance and his old poverty. A man who was the bully of humility.

A year or two younger than his eminently practical friend, Mr Bounderby looked older; his seven or eight and forty might have had the seven or eight added to it again, without surprising anybody. He had not much hair. One might have fancied he had talked it off; and that what was left, all standing up and in disorder, was in that condition from constantly being blown about by his windy boastfulness.

from Hard Times *by Charles Dickens (genre: classic novel)*

Read on!

1   How does Dickens feel about the character Mr Bounderby? How do you know?

2   What do you notice about the sentences in the second paragraph? They end with full stops, but are they really sentences? The Activity Sheet will help. Sort the 'sentences' into categories:

Clauses	Sentences containing subject and object

3   Are there any other reasons why some of these are not 'sentences'?

4   Why do you think Dickens chose to write in this way?

5   When you repeat something time and time again in a short time span, what effect does it have on your listener or reader?

6   What effect does it create about the character of Bounderby? What does it allow the author to do which he could not have done by varying the beginnings of the sentences in paragraph two?

Write on!

1   List all the details Dickens gives about the character.

Bounderby

rich, banker, merchant, manufacturer, big, loud, stared, metallic laugh ...

2   Write grammatically correct sentences using these details. For example:

Bounderby was a rich man. He was a banker, a merchant and a manufacturer. He was a big, loud man ....

3   Compare your version with that of Dickens. Yours becomes a statement of the facts, but Dickens' version creates a sense of character and his attitude towards him. In what other ways is it different?

4   Discuss how the repetition of the sentence structure helps to create this effect (compare Dickens' lines in this section with yours). What do you notice about the number of times you use the pronoun *he*? What is the effect of this?

Over to you!

Dickens creates character through laying on detail, often to the extreme. He manipulates the grammar of sentences to help him do this, often using clauses alone which only make sense in context. Write Dickensian character portraits of:

a)   a loud and aggressive football fan

b)   a shy and retiring old woman

c)   a giggling and silly schoolgirl.

Decide what details best describe these people: list adjectives. Consider how they would act, dress and behave. Start with a general statement about them. Show how you feel about them by using the same repetitious sentence pattern to reinforce the message. End with a short, final sentence in summary.

13 Making sentences interesting: phrases

*The book from which the passage comes tells the story of the island of Rum in the Inner Hebrides. Information about the island is added in **phrases** inserted into the sentences.*

A three-million-year volcanic period, some 60 million years ago, was crucial to the formation of present-day Rum. At that time this part of Scotland was an upland area, more than 500 metres high, covered with sub-tropical forests. It was a time of violent volcanic activity as the Earth's crust began to stretch and the North Atlantic Ocean began to develop. All along the western seaboard of Scotland a string of volcanoes began to erupt – Arran, Mull, Ardnamurchan, Skye, St Kilda and Rum, which was one of the first.

The thinning and rifting of the Earth's crust reduced the pressure on the solid rocks below and caused parts of them to melt, so that the liquid rock (magma) rose from depths as great as 100 km along cracks and vents in the crust towards the Earth's surface. Some of the magma poured across the landscape as lava; examples of lava pre-dating the development of the Rum volcano, representing part of the Eigg and Muck lavafields, can be seen in the Allt nam Bà area.

Other magma cooled and solidified in the vents, and was exposed millions of years later as 'dykes' and 'sills', seen now especially in the northern part of Rum along the coast between Kilmory and Guirdil, and along the south-west coast between A'Bhrìdeanach and Harris.

from Rum: Nature's Island
by Magnus Magnusson
(genre: information)

Glossary

dyke a mass of igneous (volcanic) rock which has pushed upwards through layers of other rock
sill a sheet of igneous rock parallel to the layers of other kinds of rock around it

Read on!

Much of the information in the passage is given in phrases which are added to sentences or clauses. For example, the first sentence could be reduced to *A period was crucial*. This makes grammatical sense, but gives little information.

> *A phrase is a unit within a sentence. It usually consists of more than one word. It cannot act as a sentence.*

1   Write the phrases from the first sentence in the passage which answer the following questions:
a)   To what was the period crucial?
b)   How long ago did the period occur?
c)   How long did it last?

2   The second sentence can be shortened to *This part was covered*. Write the phrases from the second sentence of the passage which answer the following questions:
a)   Of what was it part?
b)   What kind of area was it, geographically?
c)   How high was it?
d)   With what was it covered?

Write on!

1   Add phrases to the following sentence to give the information which is asked for:

Volcanoes erupted.

The sentence will increase in length as you add the information. The Activity Sheet will help.
a)   What were the volcanoes like?
b)   Did all the volcanoes erupt?
c)   How old were they?
d)   Where were they?
e)   Where can people read about them?
f)   Where else can people read about them?
g)   What did the volcanoes form as a result of erupting?
h)   What were these formations like?
i)   Where are they?

> *Re-write the sentence each time you add a phrase. Some of the information you need is in the passage; use information texts and your own knowledge of volcanoes to add the rest.*

2   a)   Write questions which can be answered by adding phrases to the following sentence:

   Rum is an island.

   b)   Add a phrase to answer each question. Re-write the sentence each time you add a phrase. The sentence will increase in length each time.

Over to you!

Plan an explanation of how something happened. This could be related to history, geography, current affairs or someone's biography.
• Begin by writing sentences which state simple facts.

• Make notes about the information which you need to add.
• Add the information to the sentences a phrase at a time. The Activity Sheet will help.

14 Making sentences interesting: clauses

*The passage is about what it was like in Hiroshima in Japan after an atomic bomb was dropped there on 6 August 1945. By building up sentences through adding **clauses**, the writer describes the scene.*

At the centre of the city we stopped and looked about us, still unable to believe that one bomb had been responsible for this holocaust. But it was not difficult, standing on this hot road in the heart of the dead city, to imagine the great flash that had first dazzled and then incinerated the shocked people of Hiroshima. Nor was it hard to imagine the immense wave of searing heat that had followed and blasted down buildings and houses like matchsticks, and that had overturned thousands and thousands of hibachis (charcoal burners), so that all over Hiroshima there sprang countless pinpoints of flame that grew with nightmare speed into the roaring furnace that engulfed the living and the dead.

And, as we stood almost ankle deep in ashes, it was not hard to imagine how those who survived the blast must have run screaming up and down this now silent street. Some would have been carrying their crying, clutching children; others half supporting, half tugging, the shocked older people; all frantically seeking to escape from the blistering, searing heat that had turned their peaceful homes into places of horror, and their familiar streets into crematoriums in which perished possessions, hopes, and, in the end, fear …

But that was imagination.

The reality was the girl with scarred features who passed with averted face. And the listless people who went by dully; the scarred people; the burnt people; the apathetic people. And the people who even now showed not the slightest sign of hostility or resentment.

Saddened and depressed beyond words at the magnitude of the tragedy, and feeling like ghouls, we decided to leave Hiroshima that same day. There was little to keep us here; nothing to see; no place to rest; nothing to eat; nothing to drink.

Fortunately for our peace of mind we knew nothing of such atomic age refinements as radiation sickness, and although we occasionally picked up a statue or kicked over a strangely fused piece of metal for a closer look, we were never tempted to take a souvenir. One does not rob a tomb.

from Road to Hiroshima
by Kenneth Harrison
(genre: report)

Read on!

The writer recounts what he saw and did. Many of the sentences have more than one clause. Each clause adds an idea or information.

A clause contains a verb.

1 Write two sentences from the passage which contain only one clause (**simple sentences**).
2 List the clauses in longer sentences which tell you about how the writer imagines:
   a) the power of the bomb
   b) the burning which took place in Hiroshima
   c) the terror of the people
   d) the effects of the bomb on the survivors.

Sentences become longer and more interesting as clauses are added to them.

3 List the information given in each of the following sentences. How is each piece of information added to the sentence?

Look for clauses and the connectives which join them.

a) Nor was it hard to imagine the immense wave of searing heat that had followed and blasted down buildings and houses like matchsticks, and that had overturned thousands and thousands of hibachis (charcoal burners), so that all over Hiroshima there sprang countless pinpoints of flame that grew with nightmare speed into the roaring furnace that engulfed the living and the dead.
b) Saddened and depressed beyond words at the magnitude of the tragedy, and feeling like ghouls, we decided to leave Hiroshima that same day.

Write on!

Re-write the passage in sentences of one clause (and therefore one verb) only, for example:

At the centre of the city we stopped.
We looked about us.
[We were] unable to believe.
One bomb had been responsible for this holocaust.

On the Activity Sheet you can practise, using different sentences.

Words made from verbs and ending in '-ing' are sometimes used as nouns or adjectives.

When you separate the clauses, some of the connectives will not be needed.

Over to you!

Plan a description of a scene after a momentous event (from history or a news report, or one you have witnessed).
a) Make notes about the scene.
b) Write simple sentences to recount the event.

c) Add clauses to each sentence giving extra information, ideas or your own thoughts.
d) Edit and redraft your work.

You could put the clauses in a different order or use different connectives.

15 Connectives

*The passage is adapted from the description and explanation of a painting; it was written to help the viewer to understand the background of the painting and what it would have meant to people at the time. Words, phrases and clauses within the sentences are linked in different ways by different types of **connective**.*

Although we once called the two ladies 'sisters', they might have been cousins, but they were certainly not identical twins. If you look closely you can see that the lady on the left has blue eyes and the one on the right has brown eyes. Each baby has eyes of the same colour as its mother and has the same material on the front of its dress as she does, so that the family connection is clearly brought out.

The picture seems to record the christening of the babies. This usually happened very soon after they were born because so many babies died very young. They are wrapped in their christening robes and their mothers are wearing decorative hoods, which you can see above the big ruff collars. These would have been worn for the ceremony. The clothes may seem much too stiff and complicated for anyone to wear in bed, but on all occasions and especially on those that marked important family and public events, people wore clothes that indicated their place in society. This tradition still exists (in the army, for instance) but in those days it affected almost everybody and a painter would have to be very careful to present the clothes accurately.

In our picture the clothes seem more important than the people wearing them. The ladies are not shown as individuals but as members of their family and rank in society. We are not told their names. They are dressed almost exactly alike and they are even sitting holding their babies in the same position, one that you can see in other pictures of mothers of the same period.

In fact the picture is not very natural, as you can tell by comparing it to the next one in this book. Like other portraits of its day it did not need to be very natural. Portraits were the most usual kind of picture. They were often hung up in large numbers in a special room (the gallery) of the great houses of the aristocrats and large landowners to show off the superiority of their family and political connections. Clothes and other indications of rank and wealth were therefore more important than naturalness.

Like many other paintings of the period, *The Cholmondeley Ladies* was painted to satisfy the client rather than the artist – he was paid to produce only what his client wanted. Some painters were very famous for their skill but this one, like many others, was a local craftsman and we do not even know his name.

from Looking at Pictures in the Tate Gallery *by Michael Compton (genre: explanation)*

Read on!

Connectives are words or phrases used to link other words, phrases and clauses in a sentence. They can also link sentences and paragraphs.

1 Identify the connective words and phrases in the passage.
2 Give an example from the passage of a sentence in which words, phrases or clauses are linked by connectives in each of the following ways:
   a) to show a simple relationship (for example, *and*, *with*, *also*, *too*, *as well as*)
   b) to show a contrast (for example, *but*, *although*)
   c) to show time (for example, *after*)
   d) to show a consequence (for example, *so*, *because*, *therefore*)
   e) to show an alternative (for example, *if*, *either*, *or*)
   f) to show comparison (for example, *as*, *like*, *than*, *more*, *less*)
   g) to show purpose (for example, *so that*, *in order to*, *to*).

> *Connectives do not have to be placed between the words, phrases or clauses they link.*

3 Re-write four sentences from the passage with a connective word or phrase in a different position without altering the meaning of the sentence.

Write on!

1 a) Re-write the passage, taking out the connective words and phrases. You will need to split up some of the sentences, for example:

   We once called the two ladies 'sisters'. They might have been cousins. They were certainly not identical twins.

   b) With a partner, discuss the changes and make notes about any changes of meaning which have resulted from them.
2 Add information from the passage to the following sentences. Use connectives.

   a) Portrait painters had to be careful to paint the details of clothing correctly.
   b) In the seventeenth century many babies died soon after they were born.
   c) Rich people liked to show off their importance and wealth.
   d) We can tell that the Cholmondeley ladies were not identical twins.
   e) One baby has blue eyes.
   f) People paid artists to paint portraits of themselves and their families.
   g) The name of the artist who painted *The Cholmondeley Ladies* is not known.

> *Use as many connectives as you need.*

Over to you!

a) Research a painting or sculpture. Find out how the artist approached it and what he or she was trying to express.
b) Make notes about the work of art and from them write simple sentences (sentences containing only one clause).
c) Use connectives to link your ideas within sentences. The Activity Sheet will help.

> *Use information texts and the websites of art galleries and local authorities.*

16   New paragraphs

*The passage is from a book which tells the stories of the inventions of everyday things. Each **paragraph** in the passage has a specific purpose or is about a particular aspect of the development of fish fingers.*

Fish Fingers

In America it remains the lowly fish stick, in Italy it is an expensive delicacy, but in Britain it has become perhaps the most popular convenience food ever. When Fish Fingers were introduced to the British nation by Birds Eye in 1955 an institution was created.

Despite the food rationing after the Second World War, Britain always had plenty of fish. It was cheap and it was nutritious and a good source of protein for growing children.

The government recommended it to the family, but children weren't that keen when it meant taking out bones and fiddling about with bits of skin on their plates. Neither did their mothers find preparing fish quite as convenient as they might wish.

It was the people at Birds Eye who turned their attention to producing fish in a form that was easily prepared, inexpensive and appealed to children. Birds Eye was the only frozen food brand in Britain in the early 1950s and they had already introduced frozen fillets of fish to the market. In America a Birds Eye team discovered an obscure frozen product called Fish Sticks – boneless, oblong pieces of fish covered in breadcrumbs ready for grilling or frying, made by Gorton's. This was the answer.

Herring was the most plentiful fish around the British Isles at the time, so Birds Eye first produced what they called the Herring Savoury, a stick-shaped portion coated in batter and breadcrumbs. For comparative test-marketing purposes they also made the same item using cod. The research showed that it was the cod version and not the Herring Savoury which people preferred. The Herring Savoury was dropped and cod Fish Fingers were born.

In 1965 Birds Eye used the new commercial television channel to establish Fish Fingers with the family. The famous Captain Birds Eye character was introduced in 1967 in a series of television commercials which has lasted for more than 30 years. The first ever radio commercial transmitted in Britain was also for Birds Eye Fish Fingers. The 60-second commercial went out from London Broadcasting on 8 October 1973 at 6.08 am.

Now Fish Fingers have become part of the British family way of life. Indeed, one of the complaints expatriates had when interviewed in Kuwait after the invasion by Iraq in 1980 which led to the Gulf War was that Fish Fingers for their children were no longer available in local supermarkets.

adapted from Century Makers:
One Hundred Clever Things We Take
For Granted Which Have Changed Our Lives
Over The Last One Hundred Years
by David Hillman and David Gibbs
(genre: information)

Read on!

1   Write a sub-heading to summarise each paragraph in the passage. What is the purpose of each paragraph?
2   With a partner, discuss the effect of moving the first sentence of each paragraph back to the end of the paragraph before. Explain why the writers organised the paragraphs as they did.
3   Investigate the ways in which the sentences in each paragraph are linked to one another. Make a note of connective words and phrases and repetition of other words (such as nouns and verbs) which are used to link one sentence to another: for example, *Despite the food rationing after the Second World War, Britain always had plenty of fish. **It** was cheap and nutritious…* (*It* refers to *fish* in the sentence before.)

> *Examples of connective words:*
> it, that, they, this, which

4   Look for the ideas which link each paragraph to the one before. Make notes about the ways in which the paragraphs follow on from one another.
5   Photocopy or scan the text, cut out the paragraphs and experiment with altering their order. Comment on the effects of the changes you make.

Write on!

1   Copy the chart. On it, write notes about the information given in the passage.

	Fish Fingers
Convenience	
Cheapness	
Nutrition	
Research	
Marketing	
History	

2   Using your notes, and without looking at the passage, write a paragraph for each heading from your chart. Write introductory and concluding paragraphs.

> *Use books and leaflets on nutrition and advertisements for, and packets from, different brands of fish fingers to find other information to add to your notes.*

3   Use logical connectives to alter the passage: emphasise the explanation of the success of fish fingers.

> *Useful logical connectives:*
> as a result, because, in order to, in that way, so, the outcome was, the result was, this meant.

Over to you!

1   Use a chart to organise information on another topic. Decide on the best headings to use. The Activity Sheet will help.
2   Write up your notes in sentences.
3   Arrange the information in each section of your chart as a paragraph, using connective words and phrases to make links between the sentences.
4   With a partner, check that there are links between the paragraphs.

> *Words such as nouns can be repeated to act as connectives.*

17   Structuring a paragraph

The writer of this biography of Paul McCartney splits the text into paragraphs on different, but connected, topics. He introduces each new topic in the first sentence of the paragraph and then develops the paragraph, linking the sentences to one another with connective words and phrases.

In 1953, out of the ninety children at Joseph Williams School who took the eleven-plus exam, Paul was one of the four who received high enough marks to qualify for a place at the Liverpool Institute, the city's top grammar school. The Institute was one of the best schools in the country and regularly sent more of its students to Oxford and Cambridge Universities than any other British state school. It was founded in 1837 and its high academic standards made it a serious rival to Eton, Harrow and the other great public schools. In 1944 it was taken over by the state as a free grammar school but its high standards as well as many of the public-school traditions still remained.

Paul first met George Harrison when they found themselves sharing the same hour-long bus ride each day to Mount Street in the city centre, and identified each other as Institute boys by their school uniforms and caps. George was born in February 1943, which placed him in the year below Paul, but because they shared the ride together Paul put their eight-month age difference to one side and George quickly became one of his best friends. Paul soon made himself at home in the welcoming front room of George's house at 25 Upton Green, a cul-de-sac one block away from Paul's house on Ardwick Road.

The little village of Hale was less than two miles away, with thatched roofs, home of the giant Childe of Hale who, legend has it, was nine foot tall. Paul and Michael [his younger brother] would stare at his grave in wonder. The worn gravestone is still there, inscribed 'Hyre lyes ye childe of Hale'. It was a favourite destination for a family walk. On the way back Paul's parents and the two boys would stop at a teashop called the Elizabethan Cottage for a pot of tea, Hovis toast and home-made jam. It was a pleasant, genteel interlude, a touch of quality before they walked back to their very different life among the grey houses and hard concrete roads of the housing estate.

'This was where my love of the country came from,' Paul said. 'I was always able to take my bike and in five minutes I'd be in quite deep countryside. I remember the Dam woods, which had millions of rhododendron bushes. We used to have dens in the middle of them because they get quite bare in the middle so you could squeeze in. I've never seen that many rhododendrons since.' Sometimes, however, rather than play with his friends, Paul preferred to be alone. He would take his *Observer Book of Birds* and wander down Dungeon Lane to the lighthouse on a nature ramble or climb over the fence and go walking in the fields.

from Paul McCartney: Many Years From Now *by Barry Miles (genre: biography)*

Read on!

1. a) What does the opening sentence of each paragraph tell you about the subject-matter of the paragraph?
    b) Write a summary of, and a sub-heading for, each paragraph.
    c) What impression does each paragraph give of the early life of Paul McCartney?

2. Write in full who or what exactly is meant by the following. Explain how you can tell from the rest of the paragraph:
    a) 'the Institute' (paragraph 1, sentence 2)
    b) 'It' and 'its' (paragraph 1, sentences 3 and 4)
    c) 'George' (paragraph 2, sentence 2)
    d) 'his grave' (paragraph 3, sentence 2)
    e) 'the worn gravestone' (paragraph 3, sentence 3)
    f) 'it' (paragraph 3, sentence 4)
    g) 'On the way back' (paragraph 3, sentence 5)
    h) 'It' (paragraph 3, sentence 6)
    i) 'them' (paragraph 4, sentence 4).

3. Investigate each paragraph. How is each detail or idea linked to those in other sentences in the paragraph?

Sentence	Details or ideas linked to other sentences	Linking words
1		

Look for connective words and phrases and repeated words.

Write on!

1. Explore the connectives in the passage. Re-write the second paragraph using different connectives to make links between the sentences. Comment on the effects you can create.

    Connectives with which you could experiment: although, at last, because, before, but, despite the fact that, even though, in case, in spite of that, on the contrary, so that, therefore, with.

2. a) Investigate the order of the sentences in each paragraph. Key in or scan the text, and rearrange each paragraph with the sentences in a different order.
    b) Make notes about the effects of changing the sentence-order. Say which order is the best, and which do not make sense, and why.

    Keep the sentences in the same paragraphs; do not move them from one paragraph to another.

Over to you!

Make notes about your memories from when you were younger.
*   Concentrate on one topic about which you can write one paragraph.
*   Re-write your notes as sentences.

*   Write an opening sentence to tell the reader what the paragraph is about.
*   Link the sentences using connectives or repetition. The Activity Sheet will help.

18 Sentence structure

D.H. Lawrence describes an unusual event on his travels. He has carefully crafted his sentences to create effects which draw the reader into the experience.

There was a slight crowding to the centre, round the lid. The old antelope-priest (so-called) was stooping. And before the crowd could realise anything else a young priest emerged, bowing reverently with the neck of a pale, delicate rattlesnake held between his teeth, the little, naïve, bird-like head of the rattlesnake quite still, near the black cheek, and the long, pale, yellowish, spangled body of the snake dangling like some thick, beautiful cord. On passed the black-faced young priest with the wondering snake dangling from his mouth, pacing in the original circle, while behind him, leaping almost on his shoulders, was the oldest heavy priest, dusting the young man's shoulders with the feather prayer sticks, in an intense, earnest anxiety of concentration such as I have only seen in the old Indian men during a religious dance.

Came another young black-faced man out of the confusion with another snake dangling and writhing from his mouth, and an elder priest dusting him from behind with the feathers: and then another, and another: till it was all confusion, probably, of six and then four young priests with snakes dangling from their mouths, going round, apparently three times in the circle. At the end of the third round the young priest stooped and delicately laid his snake on the earth, waving him away, as it were, into the world.

And after wondering a moment, the pale, delicate snake steered away with a rattlesnake's beautiful movement, rippling and looping, with the small, sensitive head lifted like an antenna, across the sand to the massed audience squatting solid on the ground around. Like soft, watery lightning went the wondering snake at the crowd. As he came nearer, the people began to shrink aside, half mesmerised.

from Mornings in Mexico *by D.H. Lawrence*
(genre: travel writing)

Read on!

1 Read the first paragraph. What do you notice about the first two sentences, compared with the third?
2 How do these first two sentences reflect the mood of the dramatic scene?
3 How does Lawrence break up the longer sentences? Copy and complete the chart:

4 The third paragraph describes the snake. How does the sentence, through its use of punctuation, give you an impression of the snake?
5 After considering these three paragraphs, decide how a sentence can have 'shape'.

Sentence	Punctuation used	Effect
'And before the crowd ... beautiful cord'	Commas	Describes everything in minute detail and slows down the description.

Write on!

1 Revise work on simple, compound and complex sentences. The Activity Sheet will help.
2 Find examples of as many simple, compound and complex sentences as you can in the passage.
3 Look at how the short, tense sentences of the first paragraph are followed by the long, twisting sentence. Write sentences of a similar length and shape in a paragraph describing the atmosphere at the beginning of a sports event: for example, the kick-off at a football match and the quick action which follows.
4 Using a similar format, describe what a theatre might be like before a comic play or pantomime: the silence or murmur of the audience followed by action, colour, lights and laughter.

Over to you!

Imagine you are watching through the window a march or a demonstration outside your school . Use the following plan to help you to write about it:

• Stage 1: Use short, tense sentences to describe the crowds forming.
• Stage 2: More people arrive and the situation becomes confusing. Use longer 'winding' sentences to give an impression of the confusion.
• Stage 3: The march begins. Write long sentences, broken by commas and minute detail, to suggest the shape and movement of the crowd.
• Stage 4: The crowd moves into the distance. Use shorter and shorter sentences as they move out of sight.

19 Extending sentences

Some kinds of writing demand simple, factual sentences. Other kinds, especially imaginative writing, need more complex sentences. In this passage the writer joins simple sentences using words such as which, as *and* but. *He makes connections between one part of the sentence and another.*

The more he tried to sleep, the more he couldn't. He tried counting sheep, which is sometimes a good way of getting to sleep, and, as that was no good, he tried counting Heffalumps. And that was worse because every Heffalump that he counted was making straight for a pot of Pooh's honey, and eating it all. For some minutes he lay there miserably, but when the five hundred and eighty-seventh Heffalump was licking its jaws, and saying to itself, 'Very good honey this, I don't know when I've tasted better,' Pooh could bear it no longer. He jumped out of bed, he ran out of the house, and he ran straight to the Six Pine Trees.

The Sun was still in bed, but there was a lightness in the sky over the Hundred Acres Wood which seemed to show that it was waking and would soon be kicking off its clothes. In the half light the Pine Trees looked cold and lonely, and the Very Deep Pit seemed deeper than it was, and Pooh's jar of honey at the bottom was something mysterious, a shape and no more. But as he got nearer to it his nose told him that it was indeed honey, and his tongue came out and began to polish up his mouth, ready for it.

'Bother!' said Pooh, as he got his nose inside the jar. 'A Heffalump has been eating it!' and then he thought a little and said, 'Oh, no, I did. I forgot.'

Indeed, he had eaten most of it. But there was a little left at the very bottom of the jar, and he pushed his head right in, and began to lick …

from Winnie the Pooh *by A.A. Milne*
(genre: children's fiction)

Read on!

1 Why are children's stories usually written in simple sentences? What effect do they create?
2 Imagine you are re-writing the story for *very* young children. Write just the information needed using simple sentences.

   He tried to sleep.
   He couldn't.
   He tried counting sheep.

3 The passage contains compound and complex sentences. Identify the connectives *which, and, because* and *but* which are used in the passage.
4 How do they help to make the sentences more interesting by extending them?

Write on!

1 The second sentence could be re-written more simply.

   He tried counting sheep. This is sometimes a good way of getting to sleep. That was no good. He tried counting Heffalumps.

   The author has used *which* and *and* to connect the statements into one sentence. What effect do the connectives have? For example, how does *which* suggest a connection between the two statements?
2 Re-write the sentence using a series of different connectives. Discuss the different meanings created.

3 At the beginning of the second paragraph the writer adds extra description using *which* to join dependent clauses. What extra information does he add? Why doesn't the writer use *who*?
4 Write five sentences using *which* to join clauses in this way. The Activity Sheet will help.
5 Continue the story for a few paragraphs, writing interesting complex sentences, but without making it too difficult for young children.

Some connectives to help:
although, because, before, in order that, since, so that, unless, while, who

Over to you!

1 Write a story for very young children to **read** for themselves, using only simple, short sentences. This could be about an animal or an event similar to the passage.
2 Re-write this story to be **told** to older children.
   • Do not change the original story.

• Use the simple sentences as the basis for your writing.
• You will need to make the sentences longer and more interesting by extending them.
• Add relevant and interesting detail when appropriate.

20 Verb tenses

In this article the writer uses mainly the present tense (to report the situation), but the past tense is also used (to recount events leading to the situation and what has been found out about it), and the future tense is used to express how the problem will be solved. Each tense is used for a purpose.

Tennis serves up homes for mice

Conservationists are hoping an endangered species of mouse will play ball in the North-East – with some help from Wimbledon.

Some of the 36,000 tennis balls used during the tournament, which starts today, have been earmarked for the Northumberland countryside as artificial homes for harvest mice. The All England Tennis Club is donating the balls to help a scheme by the Wildlife Trusts in Northumberland, Avon and Glamorgan which aims to encourage breeding in existing strongholds.

Harvest mice, which weigh only six grammes when adult – about the same as a 20p piece – are endangered because their habitat has come under threat from intensive farming.

The smallest British mammal, they normally weave homes which are the same size as a tennis ball from grass and reeds part way up long stalks.

Discarded tennis balls to be used under the scheme will have a 16 mm hole bored into them. The mice can make their nests in relative safety from predators including birds of prey and weasels.

The balls are attached to poles up to 1.5 metres off the ground in areas where harvest mice normally settle, particularly reedbeds, grassland and hedgerows. There are five colonies in Northumberland.

Dr Simon Lyster, director of the Wildlife Trusts, said, 'The harvest mouse is an excellent indicator of the health of our fields and hedgerows.

'It has been under increasing pressure, and we hope that artificial nests will provide them with the help they need to survive.'

from The Northern Echo, *25 June 2001*
(genre: non-chronological report)

Read on!

1 The passage reports the situation as it is, what has led up to it and what will happen in the future. Write the sentences or clauses which relate to each aspect of the report:

The situation as it is	What has led up to the situation	What is going to happen

2 Identify the verbs in the passage and record them on a chart.

Sentence	Verbs and tenses		
	Present	Past	Future
1	are hoping		will play
2			

3 Sometimes the future tense is expressed in ways which sound like the present.
   a) Give examples of three future tense verbs which sound like the present.
   b) Re-write the sentences making the verbs sound more like the future.

4 Find all the sentences in which there is a shift of tense (you have already identified the verbs). Explain why there is a shift of tense.

5 A non-chronological report is written mainly in the present tense. Explain why the other tenses are used.

Write on!

Tenses can be **simple** or **continuous**: simple present (*we stay*), simple past (*we stayed*) and simple future (*we shall stay*), continuous present (*we are staying*), continuous past (*we were staying*) and continuous future (*we shall be staying*). Continuous tenses are formed using auxiliary verbs such as *am, was, shall*.

Sometimes the meanings of the simple and continuous tenses are different.

1 a) Re-write the passage, changing simple tenses to continuous, and vice versa.
   b) Underline and explain any changes which affect the meanings of the sentences.

2 a) Make notes from the passage and from any other sources:

The problem facing harvest mice	The solution to the problem	How the solution will work

   b) Using your notes only, and without looking at the passage, write a report about the threat of extinction for harvest mice and possible solutions.

Over to you!

a) Make notes about a local or national problem facing people or animals.
b) Organise your notes:
   i)   the situation as it is
   ii) how it has arisen
   iii) what can be done about it.
c) Write your notes as complete sentences, taking care with tenses. The Activity Sheet will help.
d) Check the tenses. Should any simple tenses be continuous, or vice versa? Edit and redraft your report.

21 Active and passive verbs

*The writer of this newspaper report has used both **active** and **passive** verbs.*
Sometimes either form could have been used, but sometimes the passive is used
where the agent of the verb is not known or is not important.

DRAGON ATTACKS STAR'S HUSBAND

By Sarah Getty

Sharon Stone's husband was recovering in hospital last night after being attacked by a dragon during a family outing to the zoo.

The *Basic Instinct* star looked on as a Komodo dragon – a 10ft-long Indonesian lizard – pounced on 48-year-old Phil Bronstein.

The couple and their one-year-old son, Roan, were being taken on a private tour of a Los Angeles zoo as a Father's Day treat.

A keeper invited Bronstein, who had always wanted to see a Komodo dragon, to join him in the reptile's cage. The keeper suggested he remove his tennis shoes because the lizard might mistake them for his next meal – white rats.

But, as soon as Bronstein entered the enclosure, the reptile seized his foot with its sharp-toothed jaws.

Sharon Stone, 43, said, 'It was horrifying. I was standing on the outside and couldn't do anything. The beast clamped down on Phil's foot and thrashed its body around.'

Bronstein, executive editor of the *San Francisco Chronicle*, managed to prise open the dragon's jaws before escaping through a small feeding door in the cage.

He underwent emergency surgery to reattach several severed tendons and rebuild his big toe, which was crushed by the reptile's jaws.

The dragon was placed in quarantine after the attack.

Sharon Stone said, 'We certainly don't blame the people at the zoo.'

Komodo dragons, which feed on small mammals and are known to be aggressive, are worth up to £20,000 on the black market.

The zoo owns two dragons which were confiscated from smugglers.

from Metro
(genre: newspaper report)

Read on!

1   Identify the verbs in each sentence and decide if they are active or passive, and, if it is included in the sentence, make a note of the subject of each verb.

The subject of an active verb does something. The subject of a passive verb has something done to it. Sometimes the subject of a verb is not included in the sentence.

Sentence	Active verb	Subject	Passive verb	Subject
1	was recovering	Sharon Stone's husband	being attacked	Sharon Stone's husband

The Activity Sheet gives some practice.

2   a)   Make a note of the agent of each verb (if known). Notice the use of the word *by* to link the agent to a passive verb. You could write your notes on a chart:

Sentence	Active verb	Agent	Passive verb	Agent (if known)
1	was recovering	Sharon Stone's husband	being attacked	a dragon

The agent of a verb (whether active or passive) is the person or thing which carries out the action.

b)   Compare your chart with the one on which you recorded the subjects of the verbs.

3   List the auxiliary verbs used to create the passive verbs (see page 43).

4   Explain why the writer has chosen the active or passive form of each verb.

Sometimes the passive is used where the agent – the person (or thing) who (or which) does the action – is not important.

Write on!

Sometimes active clauses and sentences can be written in the passive and vice versa.

1   Re-write the passage in two versions:
a)   making the verbs active, where possible
b)   making the verbs passive, where possible.

2   Compare the subjects and agents of the verbs with those in the charts in **Read on! 1** and **2**.

3   Describe the effects of each of the two versions.

Keep the meaning the same. For example, in the first sentence it would be wrong to write after attacking a dragon, *but correct to write* after a dragon had attacked him.

Over to you!

Write a recount of an event in the style of the newspaper report.

•   Write mainly in the past tense.
•   Experiment with active and passive verbs and decide which works best in each sentence:

–   Consider the importance of the agent of the verb.
–   Consider the effect of active and passive verbs across whole paragraphs.

22 Using speech marks

Two characters meet in a Florida bar.

Direct speech *is what someone says. The actual words spoken are shown by placing them inside speech marks. Paragraphing speech also allows the reader to understand the conversation.*

"Aren't you Richard Gordon?"

"Yes."

"I'm Herbert Spellman. We met at a party in Brooklyn one time, I believe."

"Maybe," said Richard Gordon. "Why not?"

"I liked your last book very much," said Spellman. "I liked them all."

"I'm glad," said Richard Gordon. "Have a drink?"

"Have one with me," said Spellman. "Have you tried this *ojen*?"

"It's not doing me any good."

"What's the matter?"

"Feeling low."

"Wouldn't try another?"

"No. I'll have whisky."

"You know, it's something to me to meet you," Spellman said. "I don't suppose you remember me at that party?"

"No. But maybe it was a good party. You're not supposed to remember a good party, are you?"

"I guess not," said Spellman. "It was Margaret Van Brunt's. Do you remember?" he asked hopefully.

"I'm trying to."

"I was the one set fire to the place," Spellman said.

"No," said Gordon.

"Yes," said Spellman, happily. "That was me. That was the greatest party I was ever on."

from To Have and Have Not
*by Ernest Hemingway
(genre: modern fiction)*

Read on!

1 How many characters are speaking? How do you know?
2 How does this show that it is important to paragraph speech correctly?
3 Do we get any sense of where the characters are? What clues are given?
4 How much information do we learn about each character? If the narrator is not giving this information, how do we know it?
5 Which is the more interesting way of conveying information: the narrator telling you directly or the reader picking up essential pieces during the natural process of reading the text?
6 Look closely at the punctuation of the first five lines of the passage. Make a list of essential information necessary for 'How to punctuate direct speech'. The Activity Sheet will help.

Write on!

1 Re-write the first five lines of the passage as a playscript.

SPELLMAN: Aren't you Richard Gordon?
GORDON: Yes.

   - What do you need to change about the punctuation and layout?
   - What are the different audiences and purposes of each of these pieces of writing?

2 Hemingway used the simplest language possible in his writing to achieve the effect of maximum realism. This meant he used *said* as the only verb to describe a person's speech. Use a thesaurus to find other verbs you could substitute in this passage. Re-write the passage.

'Maybe,' shouted Richard Gordon.

3 Discuss the effect of changing the verb on the meaning and characters in the story.
4 Continue the dialogue, using the same style as Hemingway does.
5 Introduce a third character into the dialogue and change the location. What changes will be necessary to ensure that your reader is aware of who is speaking and what the person is like?

Over to you!

Write a conversation between two or three friends, out together for a fun night in a club.
   - Use a similar sparse style to Hemingway's.
   - Be real in the way the characters speak and how you write this.
   - Punctuate and paragraph the speech appropriately.
   - Use only *said* to identify what the speakers say.
   - Keep the narrator out of your writing. This means you need to convey all necessary detail in the words of the speakers themselves.

23 Non-chronological report

Reports are written to describe or classify. They organise and record information. To fulfil their aim, they use specific language features. Reports such as this one, used in geography, give us information in a particular order, but that sequence has nothing to do with time order (chronological order).

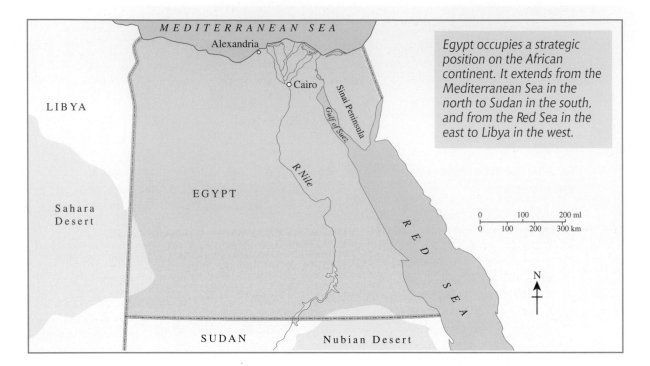

Egypt occupies a strategic position on the African continent. It extends from the Mediterranean Sea in the north to Sudan in the south, and from the Red Sea in the east to Libya in the west.

EGYPT

Area
Even though the total surface area is about one million square kilometres, less than 5% of the land is inhabited. The total area is 1,001,450 square km. The land area is 995,450 square km.

Population
Due to the concentration of the population in the Nile Valley and the Delta region, the population density rate is 64.9/km² in the total area. According to the 1996 census, nearly 43% of the total urban population live in Cairo (the capital) and Alexandria. Cairo, the largest city in Africa, has a population of 6.79 million. The total population is 59,272,382, including an estimated 2.2 million residing abroad. The population is growing at the rate of one million every eight months, which would give Egypt a population of more than 68 million by the turn of the century.

Climate
Egypt has a frost-free climate which allows for year-round farming. It receives only half an inch of rain per year on average. Temperatures are excessively hot, ranging up to 60°C in the summer. Prevailing winds blow to the south from the Mediterranean.

Topography
Egypt is protected by natural boundaries on all sides: the Mediterranean Sea to the north; the Sahara Desert to the west; the Nubian Desert and Swamps to the south, and the Red Sea and Sinai Peninsula to the east. It consists of a vast desert plateau interrupted by the Nile valley and delta.

Economic activity
The main industrial activities include textiles, food processing, tourism, chemicals, petroleum, construction, cement and metals.

The most important agricultural products are cotton, rice, corn, wheat, beans, fruit and vegetables.

Imports and exports
Imports total $11.2 billion per year. These include machinery and equipment, foods, fertilisers, wood products and durable consumer goods. Total exports total $3.1 billion per year. These include crude oil and petroleum products, cotton yarn, raw cotton, textiles, metal products and chemicals.

Read on!

1 Where would you be likely to find a report such as this?
2 What would be its purpose and its audience?
3 Identify the features of a non-chronological report. The Activity Sheet will help.
4 Why does this report use sub-headings? How do they help to organise the information?

5 How do other layout features make the information easier for the reader to assimilate? Copy and complete the chart.

Layout feature	Example from the text
Large typefaces for titles	
Different typefaces for different purposes	
The use of bold typefaces	
Maps and diagrams	

Write on!

1 Re-write the first three sections, changing the present to the past tense.
   - How does the meaning of the text change?
   - What is the effect of this?
   - Is the report still suitable for its purpose?
2 A chronological report is one which takes a particular time scheme as its structure. The best example of this is a biography. Produce a detailed time line for your own life so far, and write a report about your own life using sub-headings.
   - Which tense will you use?
   - Which of the other features identified earlier will not be appropriate?
3 Choose another country which you are studying in geography. Write a report using the correct features of style and grammar as identified for its purpose and audience.

Over to you!

Write a report on the development of a popular sport: for example, basketball or skateboarding. You may have to do some research.
- If you use the Internet, do not just copy the information; think of the main features you want to communicate and use these for your sub-headings.
- Make notes and then re-write these in your own words, but using the features identified here.
- Provide a general opening, use the present tense and the third person, use an objective, general style and subject-specific, specialised terminology.

24 Recount

This is from an information book about the story of the Taj Mahal and Shah Jahan, the Mughal Emperor who had it built. 'Time' connectives are used in this chapter, which is a recount of the death of Mumtaz Mahal.

Late in December 1631 a solemn and grand funeral procession arrived in the city of Agra. There were elephants decorated with gold and silver cloths and cavalrymen with flags, riding their fine horses. Leading the procession was the fifteen-year-old Prince Shah Shuja with Wazir Khan, the Royal Physician, and Sati-un-nissa, the Head Stewardess of the Royal Household. They rode in howdahs on the backs of elephants and wore the white clothes of mourning. In the funeral bier at the centre of the procession was the body of Empress Mumtaz Mahal, mother of Prince Shuja and beloved wife of Shah Jahan, ruler of the Mughal empire.

Six months earlier, Mumtaz Mahal had died in childbirth at Bhurhanpur, about 700 kilometres south of Agra. Despite being heavily pregnant, she had accompanied Shah Jahan on a military campaign, as was her custom. Stricken with grief at her death, the emperor ordered his entire kingdom into mourning. According to Muslim practice, Mumtaz Mahal's body was buried immediately in Bhurhanpur. Six months later, it was brought to the capital, Agra, to rest in a temporary crypt in a leafy grove on the banks of the Yamuna River.

Emperor Shah Jahan had chosen the most lovely site for his wife's final resting-place. But his plans to commemorate her were grander still. Mumtaz Mahal's tomb was to be encased in a building of breathtaking beauty, an eternal monument to an eternal love: the Taj Mahal.

from The Taj Mahal
by Christine Moorcroft
(genre: historical writing)

Read on!

1 List the events which took place in the passage in a flow chart like this. Leave space to add information about the events.

> Read the whole passage to find out what happened first, and then make notes about the events, in the order in which they happened.

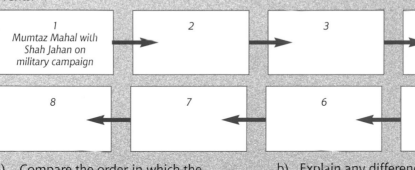

| 1 Mumtaz Mahal with Shah Jahan on military campaign | 2 | 3 | 4 |
| 8 | 7 | 6 | 5 |

2 a) Compare the order in which the events happened with the order in which they are recounted in the passage.

b) Explain any differences: why has the writer recounted the events in this order?

c) How are connectives and changes of tense used to make the order of events clear? Give examples.

Write on!

1 The sentences in the passage contain phrases describing each event. In the appropriate section of your flow chart, write the phrase from the passage which answers each question.

a) When did the funeral procession arrive?

b) Where did it arrive?

c) What was it like?

d) Who led the procession?

e) In what did the leaders ride?

2 Write ten other questions about the events in the passage. Add the answers to your flow chart.

Over to you!

Make notes about something from history.
- Use a flow chart.
- List the events in chronological order. Decide which would be the most interesting event with which to begin. Use a flow chart. The Practice and Extension Sheet will help.

- Add information about each event (see **Unit 13 Making sentences interesting: phrases** and **Unit 14 Making sentences interesting: clauses**).
- Write your recount, using your plan to help you.

> Use information texts for your research.

25 Instructions

Instructions help the reader to achieve a task or to fulfil an aim. To do this they use specific language features.

TO GET THE BEST FROM YOUR VIDEO RECORDER

How to insert the batteries into the remote control

1 Remove the cover from the back of the remote control. To do this, press the sides of the cover together and, simultaneously, slide it down.

2 Insert the batteries as indicated into the battery compartment and close the cover.

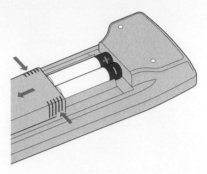

Note
- **Do not use rechargeable batteries in this remote control**
- **For the remote control to function properly, you must always point it directly at the set.**

Connecting to the aerial

You can use the auxiliary aerial supplied or connect the set to your aerial installation.

1 Insert the aerial into the socket as shown.

2 If you use the auxiliary aerial supplied, push the aerial into the mounting on the back panel until it snaps shut. Rotate the aerial until you achieve the best picture quality.

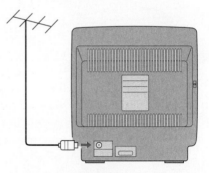

Connecting to the mains power supply

1 Insert the plug of the mains cable into the wall socket.

2 Switch the set on. The power switch is located on the left side panel of the set.

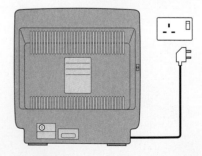

Note
- **We advise you, from now on, to switch the set to standby using the standby button on the front of the set or on the remote control. When the set is in the standby mode, a small red lamp on the left of the set will be lit.**

Read on!

1 Where would you be likely to find instructions such as these?
2 What would be their purpose and audience?
3 Identify the features of instructions. The Activity Sheet will help.

4 Why do these instructions use diagrams and boxes? How do they help to organise the information?
5 Identify other layout features which make the information easier for the reader to assimilate.

Write on!

1 Re-write the numbered instructions from the passage in the third person and the past tense to recount how someone carried out the instructions: for example, *Chris removed the cover* ....
   - How does the meaning of the text change?
   - What are the other effects of making this change of tense and person?
   - Are the instructions still suitable for their original purpose? Why?
2 Imagine you need to give the final instructions, *Connecting to the mains power supply*, over the phone to someone who is learning English. You have no access to diagrams and the person may not understand the consequences of many of the actions you need to tell him or her about. The actions could be very dangerous, so you have to think carefully about what you say. Write the instructions you would give.
   - What terms might the person not understand: for instance, *mains cable*, *left*? How can you describe these so that he or she understands?
   - Make notes about all the stages necessary.
   - Number your points so that you know you have not missed out an important stage.
   - Use the features discussed above.

Over to you!

Choose a simple procedure which you carry out often at school. Think about giving someone instructions for doing this: for instance, how to copy a file on to a computer disk.
   - Choose your audience. Is it someone younger? Someone not very confident with technology?
   - Make notes about all the stages necessary.

   - Avoid using technical language which may not be clear to the audience.
   - Number your points so that you know you have not missed out an important stage.
   - Include diagrams if they would help.
   - Write a set of instructions using the correct features of style and grammar.

26 Explanations

This article combines a recount of a scientific investigation with an explanation of the results. It was written for the BASF/Daily Telegraph Young Science Writer Awards and won second prize in the senior section.

Without a doubt, the most revelatory moment of my short scientific career was discovering that earthworms go up rather than down.

I spent an entire year studying moles. The logistics of studying an animal that rarely sticks its head above the ground, in a capital city, with a research budget of five pounds, are not to be laughed at. As every golf-course manager knows, moles dig long systems of tunnels under the ground and molehills are the irritating result. Being fairly useless above ground and almost blind, moles rarely leave the safety of their tunnel networks, feeding mostly on stray earthworms that have fallen into the tunnels and become trapped.

Earthworms are not stupid, however; if there is one thing they are good at, it is wriggling about in soil. So why, on finding themselves falling into an unfamiliar hole in the ground, would they just lie about for hours waiting to get snapped up by a hungry mole?

This puzzled me for several months, and I devised numerous experiments to try to find an answer. Eventually, I found some moles living around a reservoir several miles from Cardiff, and for months I cycled up there nearly every day with huge gardening tools strapped to my back, getting soaked to the skin and being regularly tormented by local children.

A worm expert told me that earthworms live in the bottom of long burrows in the soil, coming up to the surface to feed at night. Much later on, I realised that this was the key to the puzzle. Worms are not falling into the tunnels; instead, moles are digging straight through the worm burrows. At night the worms travel up to feed on the surface, but find themselves in the moles' tunnel, which they assume to be the ground surface, so they start to feed or wriggle around inside the tunnel. The moles are sneakily tricking the worms into a false sense of security by exploiting their natural behaviour patterns.

Another puzzling aspect of mole behaviour remained unsolved. The common myth that moles eat nothing but earthworms was not substantiated by the evidence, which revealed that they were eating any soil animal they came across. Moles create 'stores' of food that are always found to contain a single species of earthworm, the fat common ones, which have the unique feature of regrowable heads. The mole bites off their heads, leaving them paralysed but alive so that they can be stored for months until they are either eaten or they grow a new head and wriggle away. Moles are so well adapted to life in a confined space that rather than grow bigger or faster, they have evolved their behaviour to exploit neatly the behaviour of their prey.

from 'Grubbing in the mud'
by Katharine Dart
(genre: scientific writing)

Read on!

1. The explanations in the passage are contained in a recount of the research which led to them. Explanations are written in the present tense and recounts are written in the past tense.
   - Which sections of the passage are part of the recount and which are part of the explanation?
   - Write your answers on a chart:

Recount sections		Explanation sections	
From	**To**	**From**	**To**
Without a doubt, the most revelatory moment ...	... an entire year studying moles	The logistics of studying an animal ...	

2. The connectives used in recounts are of a different type from those used in an explanation.
   a) List the connectives used in the recount sections of the passage.

   *See **Unit 15 Connectives**.*

   b) List the connectives used in the explanation sections.
   c) Comment on the main difference between the two lists of connectives.

3. Comment on any differences you notice between the style of language of the recount and explanation sections of the passage.

   Think about personal and impersonal language.

Write on!

1. a) Re-write the explanation sections of the passage so that they become part of the recount. You will need to alter the verb tenses and the connectives.
   b) Comment on the differences between the purposes of a recount and an explanation and how these affect the way in which each is written.

2. a) Re-write the explanation sections of the passage as instructions for a mole on how to find, collect and store food.

   *See **Unit 25 Instructions**.*

   b) Comment on any changes you made, for example, to the verbs, connectives and layout.

Over to you!

Read through any notes you have made about an experiment or investigation you have carried out in science lessons. Plan a recount of how you carried out the experiment or investigation and of the results, and an explanation of the results.
- Base your writing on the style of the passage. You could combine the recount and the explanation in a similar way, rather than separating them.
- Think about the style of language you will use.

- Think about the verb tenses you will use in each section of your writing.
- Make a list of useful connectives: (a) for recounts (time connectives: for example, *first, for some time* and *in the end*) and (b) for explanations (connectives which express causes or logic: for example, *because, so* and *in this way*). The Practice and Extension Sheet will help.

27 **Persuasion**

5 simple steps to take action

1 GET angry at what companies, governments and individuals are doing to your world.

2 RECYCLE this paper by using it to join Greenpeace now and help stop the destruction.

3 USE the form inside to give your support, whether by Direct Debit, card or cheque.

4 SEND it back to us today. The sooner you do it, the sooner we make a difference.

5 IF you have any doubts, read on. Then follow steps 1–4. After all, if people like you won't help Greenpeace, who will?

Help save the only world we've got

A flailing dolphin gasps madly for air. Where once there was living forest, now silence reigns. More and more of our children are choked by invisible poisons. Fields of genetically modified crops dominate the countryside, bereft of song and life…

This is not science fiction. It's a realistic vision of a world without Greenpeace. It's a frightening prospect. And it's why we need your regular support today.

Think about it for a moment

If Greenpeace wasn't there to stop environmental destruction, who else would be there? Who else could put enough pressure on multinational giants such as Shell to make them change their minds? Who else could get major food manufacturers like Unilever to remove GM ingredients from their products? Who else could force a president to stop a nuclear test?

Or put it another way: if Greenpeace can't take action to protect our world, who do you think will? We can do nothing without people like you – and your regular support is vital to our work. If you can give just £3 or £4 per month by Direct Debit, we shall have a source of income we can rely on all year round. Believe me we shall use it wisely.

Just think what you could do

You could help **prevent the dolphins dying**. In 1991 we won a UN ban on high seas drift-netting, and in 1998 a ban in European waters was agreed. Thousands of dolphins will be saved from an untimely death. But we must maintain pressure so that the new ban comes into effect by the end of 2001.

Your support could be part of the money we need to **let the forests live again**. We are striving to protect the Amazon rainforest from illegal logging before it is too late.

You could even help us **prevent catastrophic changes to our climate**. Greenpeace is campaigning to stop exploration for new oil because we can burn only a quarter of known oil reserves before causing disastrous changes to the Earth's climate. We are also pushing for the greater use of clean energy solutions, like offshore wind, wave and solar power.

Then do it

So if you have ever thought of yourself as a supporter of the environment, please recycle this form – compete the Direct Debit section and send it back to us today. Because we've only got one world – and it's much better to stop the damage before it happens than to try to repair it. Can you think of a better way to spend £3 or £4 per month?

adapted from a promotional leaflet distributed by Greenpeace
(genre: persuasion)

Read on!

1 How does the cover of the leaflet attract the reader's attention? The headline is ambiguous; explain what it appears to mean at first and the meaning which you discover later in the text. How does this encourage the reader to read on?

2 What are the key points which are made in the leaflet? How did you identify the key points? Explain how they are emphasised.

Notice the use of layout and other textual effects.

3 What kind of people are the intended audience of the leaflet? How can you tell?

Look for clues to the age-range and interests of the audience.

4 Is the language of the leaflet personal or impersonal? How can you tell?

Write the phrases, clauses or sentences from the leaflet which are used to appeal to the known interests and concerns of the audience.

5 Comment on the way in which the leaflet makes logical appeals to readers by:
a) using statements of facts
b) using contrast
c) using conditionals and the consequences which show causes and effects: for instance, *if* ...
d) using repetition
e) using questions
f) using personal language in the second person: for instance, *You could* ....

6 Identify any imperative (command) forms of verbs which are used, and describe their effect.

Write on!

1 a) With a partner, plan how to re-write the passage as a non-chronological report giving information about Greenpeace.
   b) Write the non-chronological report, giving it a heading, an introductory paragraph and a summary.

2 Comment on the differences between the original passage and your altered version.

Write in the present tense and the third person. Do not use imperatives or conditionals. Use connectives to link ideas. Give examples.

Over to you!

Plan a persuasive text to encourage others in your school to support an organisation or event which you think is worthwhile. The Practice and Extension Sheet will help.
• List the main points you want to make.
• Collect information to support each point.
• Make notes on what you know about the interests and values of the audience.

• Present your persuasive text in the form of a leaflet.
• Use sub-headings and bold text.
• Think of an eye-catching headline.
• Include: statements of facts; conditionals and consequences showing causes and effects; questions; personal language in the second person; and imperatives.

28 Discursive writing

A discussion presents one or more points of view and the writer's own opinion is usually made clear, but there is no attempt to persuade others or to argue a point.

Race wars: are our schools to blame?

Are Britain's cities now condemned to their own version of 'the Troubles' in Northern Ireland? Bradford, at least, is beginning to look alarmingly like Belfast, said *The Sunday Times*. Last week, more than 100 police officers were injured in Bradford amid a hail of bricks and petrol bombs. Indeed, the police came 'dangerously close' to losing control of the city. What has turned Bradford and other northern hot spots into battle zones?

Some blame the violence on the Rude Boys, said Faisal Islam in *The Observer*. These are the young Asian men 'who zip up and down the M62 in souped-up BMWs responding to the tiniest text message hinting of trouble in the north'. But that is just one aspect of a far wider problem: the fact that so many young men in these northern towns, white or Asian, find themselves with no prospect of a job. So they 'drift into the general pattern common to disaffected British males: crime, drugs, and assorted forms of yobbery'. But an independent inquiry led by Lord Herman Ouseley, former head of the Commission for Racial Equality, has come to a rather different conclusion, said

Leo McKinstry in the *Daily Mail*. He points the finger at the city's misguided segregationist policies. Weak political leaders, he said, have 'kowtowed' to self-styled community leaders who wanted their children schooled separately, often with English as a second language.

I made the same point 15 years ago, said Ray Honeyford, a former headmaster of a Bradford school. But instead of being listened to, I was sacked for being 'a racist'. My crime was to have declared that English should be established as the basic language of education and that Bradford's policy of 'multi-culturalism' in education would lead to educational and social apartheid. But the council insisted, and still does,

that children from different ethnic groups should be given an education that suited their own particular background; that no attempt should be made to persuade immigrants to adopt British ways and that English history and traditions should not be emphasised. The results have been only too predictable: 'if you are regularly reminded at school that you are not primarily British, and that you owe your first loyalty to a land thousands of miles away, you are likely to grow up with confused ideas about who you are and frustration about where you belong'. Bradford's education polices have created a 'patchwork of conflicting ethnicities' and we are now reaping the whirlwind.

from The Week, *21 July 2001*
(genre: discussion)

Read on!

1   What topic is being discussed in the passage?
2   What contrasting points of view are discussed? Record them on a chart:

Point of view	Contrasting point of view

3   Draw a flow chart and on it write a summary of each point of view or opinion expressed in the passage. Draw arrows to show the links between them:

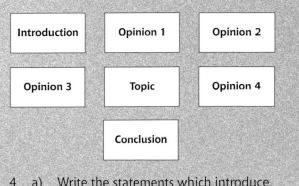

4   a)   Write the statements which introduce each point of view. What questions do they each raise in your mind?
    b)   Read the sentences which follow these statements and comment on how they clarify the statements.

Write on!

1   a)   Identify the connectives which link the paragraphs in the passage.
    b)   Identify the connectives which link the sentences in the second and third paragraphs of the passage.
2   What is the main tense in which the passage is written? Give examples.

3   a)   Make notes about the facts in the passage.
    b)   Using your notes, write a recount of the events which have taken place in Bradford.

Think about the tense and connectives you will use.

Over to you!

Make notes about an issue about which people have different opinions.
•   On a chart, write the opinions, and balance each of them with a contrasting opinion.
•   Make notes of the evidence or examples to support each opinion.
•   Use a flow chart to organise into paragraphs the contrasting opinions (and the evidence and examples to support them) about each point. The Practice and Extension Sheet will help.

•   Use logical connectives to link the opinions and to link the paragraphs.
•   Think about an opening statement to introduce each opinion and then a way of linking it to the evidence and examples you have collected.
•   Write a report in the style of the passage, beginning with an introductory paragraph which asks questions to set the scene for the discussion.
•   Write a summary sentence or paragraph in which you make your views clear.

29 Standard English

Education is, as far as I have been able to ascertain, more widely extended among street children than it was twelve or fifteen years ago. The difficulty in arriving at any conclusion on such a subject is owing to the inability to find anyone who knew, or could even form a tolerably accurate judgment of what was the state of education among these juveniles even twelve years back …

I now give the answers I received from two boys. The first, his mother told me, was the best scholar at his school when he was there, and before he had to help her in street sale. He was a pale, and not at all forward boy, of thirteen or fourteen …

Another boy, perhaps a few months older, gave me his notion of men and things. He was a thick-limbed, red-cheeked fellow; answered very freely, and sometimes, when I could not help laughing at his replies, laughed loudly himself, as if he entered into the joke.

Yes, he had heer'd of God, who made the world. Couldn't exactly recollec' when he'd heer'd on him, but he had, most sarten-ly. Didn't know when the world was made, or how anybody could do it. It must have taken a long time. It was afore his time, "or yourn either, sir." Knew there was a book called the Bible … Never heer'd tell on the deluge; of the world having been drownded; it couldn't; for there wasn't enough water to do it. He weren't a-going to fret hisself for such things as that. Didn't know what happened to people after death, only that they was buried. Had seen a dead body laid out; was a little afeared at first; poor Dick looked so different, and when you touched his face, he was so cold! oh, so cold! Had heer'd on another world; wouldn't mind if he was there hisself, if he could do better, for things was often queer here. Had heered on it from a tailor – such a clever cove, a stunner – as went to 'Straliar (Australia), and heer'd him say he was going into another world. Had never heer'd of France, but had heer'd of Frenchmen; there wasn't half a quarter so many on 'em as of Italians, with their earrings like flash gals. Didn't dislike foreigners, for he never saw none. What was they? Had heer'd of Ireland. Didn't know where it was, but it couldn't be very far, or such lots wouldn't come from there to London. Should say they walked it, aye, every bit of the way, for he'd seen them come in, all covered with dust. Had heer'd of people going to sea, and had seen the ships in the river, but didn't know nothing about it, for he was very seldom that way. The sun was made of fire, or it wouldn't make you feel so warm. The stars was fire, too, or they wouldn't shine. They didn't make it warm, they was too small. Didn't know any use they was of. Didn't know how far they was off; a jolly lot higher than the gas lights some on 'em was. Was never in a church; had heer'd they worshipped God there; didn't know how it was done; had heer'd singing and playing inside when he'd passed; never was there, for he hadn't no togs to go in, and wouldn't be let in among such swells as he had seen coming out. Was a ignorant chap, for he'd never been to school, but was up to many a move, and didn't do bad. Mother said he would make his fortin yet.

from London Labour and the London Poor, *by Henry Mayhew (genre: sociological report from the past – mid-nineteenth century)*

Glossary

cove man, chap
sarten-ly certainly
togs clothes

Read on!

1 Identify the different types of non-standard English in the passage:

Non-agreement between verbs and their subjects	Non-standard past tenses	Double negatives	Non-standard use of 'a' and 'an'	Dialect or slang expressions

2 List any words which have been spelled in non-standard ways to give an idea of the way in which the boy pronounced them.

Write the standard English versions of these words:

Non-standard spellings	Standard English spellings

3 Describe the differences between the parts of the passage which recount what the boy said and the writer's comments. Notice the differences between the styles of language, including standard and non-standard English, spelling and vocabulary.

Write on!

1 Make notes about what the boy said to Henry Mayhew, the interviewer. Record the information in standard English, but in note form.

2 From your notes, write a report about what the boy said, but in the style of the first three paragraphs.

Write in standard English and in a formal, impersonal style, using the same type of vocabulary as did Henry Mayhew.
Use a dictionary and a thesaurus.

3 Comment on the differences between this version and the original and explain why Henry Mayhew wrote it as he did.

Over to you!

Work with a partner or in a group. You will need a television set and video-recorder or a radio and cassette recorder.

Record a television programme or listen to a radio programme in which non-standard English is used.

- Make notes about the form of non-standard English which is used (including non-agreement of verbs and nouns or pronouns, double negatives, non-standard use of pronouns, dialect or slang words and non-standard pronunciation).

- Transcribe a section of the dialogue, spelling it in a way which indicates how the words are pronounced.
- Write another version in standard English for comparison.
- Read both versions aloud and comment on the differences.
- Give examples of (a) texts in which non-standard English can be more useful than standard English and (b) texts in which standard English should be used. Explain your answers.

30 Book reviews

The cool-reads review team make their reviews easy to follow by using standardised sub-headings.

The Black Dogs of Doom
by Anthony Masters

Bloomsbury, 2001, 258 pp, ISBN 0 7475 5081 6

How easy was it to get stuck into this book?

This book is not very exciting initially, but the action soon increases and you find yourself enjoying it a lot more than you would have thought. The book is very tense, and has a lot of magical content. The way the book is written suggests that there is magic all around us, except most people can't see it.

Who is it about?

The main person in the story is Si, which is a shorter version of Simon. The book makes comparisons with another boy who lived long before, although not much is heard about him, except that he lived on an island called the Ness, where the people had enemies called the Caliban.

What's the storyline?

The Caliban broke away from the Ness island early on in its history. They went to live in a place called Doom, taking the knowledge of weather spells with them. The weather spells eventually unleashed themselves on the Ness, destroying it totally. The spells had come from the *Spellbinder*, a book completed by the elders of the island. However they didn't have one spell from the *Spellbinder* – the secret to immortality. This resided on the last page. All this is told in the first few chapters, and Si learns it through dreams. It seems he is the new guardian, and the anniversary of the destruction of Ness is approaching.

How is it written?

Once you overcome the magical stuff, the book is very readable.

And the overall cool-reads verdict is

★★★★★

Really good – recommended

Other books we know about by this author

Wicked. The author has written quite a lot more.

a review by Chris Cross, aged 14, from the cool-reads team,
www.cool-reads.co.uk (genre: review)

Read on!

1 What features of the review make it easy for the reader to:
   a) decide whether or not to buy the book or borrow it from library?
   b) find it in a bookshop or library?

2 a) What does the review tell you about specific aspects of the book? Write your answers on a chart:

Genre	
Storyline	
Characters	
Setting	
Language style	
How interesting or exciting It Is	
Readers for whom it is suitable	

   b) Comment on any aspects of it which you think are missing or incomplete and about which you would like information

3 Comment on how much the writer tells you about the plot. Is it enough to interest the reader without giving away too much about the story?

4 Make a note of, and explain, all the technical vocabulary (including abbreviations) about books which is used in the review. *Use a dictionary.*

5 Identify the audience of the review. What clues told you this?

6 a) In which person is the review written? Is it the same throughout? If not, where does it change?
   b) Is the language personal or impersonal? Give examples.
   c) Compare this with book reviews in newspapers and comment on any differences in language.
   d) Why do you think the writer has chosen to write in this style?

Write on!

1 With a partner, discuss, and make notes about, any changes you would make in the style of the review if it were for a different audience: for instance, teachers.

2 Re-write the review in a formal, impersonal style.

3 Compare the new version with the original. Which do you prefer, and why?

Think about person, vocabulary and verb forms such as imperative (command), interrogative (questioning), passive and conditional.

Over to you!

Plan a review of a book you have read. The Activity Sheet will help.
- Word-process your review.
- Use a similar layout to the passage.
- Use a similar style to the passage.
- Use similar questions/sub-headings to the passage.
- Add any 'question' headings you think are missing (see **Read on! 2 (b)**).
- Include information about genre, storyline, characters and setting.
- Give information about the publisher, ISBN, number of pages and date of publication.
- Remember to give the book an overall verdict and to say for which audience it is suitable.
- Print your review, display it on your school website or e-mail it to a friend or to www.cool-reads.co.uk.

Acknowledgements

Text sources and acknowledgements

Unit 3: from C. Day Lewis, *The Otterbury Incident* (Puffin, 1970), reprinted by permission of The Random House Group Ltd; **Unit 4**: from William Gibson, *The Miracle Worker* (Bantam Books, 1984); **Unit 5**: John Clare, 'Pleasant Sounds' from *Madrigals and Chronicles*, edited by Edmund Blunden (Beaumont Press, 1924); **Unit 6**: from William Golding, *Pincher Martin* (Faber & Faber, 1956), reprinted by permission of the publisher; **Unit 10**: from Aidan MacFarlane and Ann McPherson, *The New Diary of a Teenage Health Freak* (Oxford University Press, 1987), © Aidan MacFarlane and Ann McPherson, 1987, reprinted by permission of the publisher; **Unit 11**: from Michael Heseltine, *Life in the Jungle: My Autobiography* (Hodder & Stoughton, 2000), reprinted by permission of the publisher; **Unit 13**: from Magnus Magnusson, *Rum: Nature's Island* (Luath Press, 1997), reprinted by permission of the author; **Unit 14**: from Kenneth Harrison, *Road to Hiroshima* (Rigby Publishing, 1983); **Unit 15**: from Michael Compton, *Looking at Pictures in the Tate Gallery* (Tate Gallery Publishing, 1979), reprinted by permission of Tate Enterprises; **Unit 16**: from David Hillman and David Gibbs, *Century Makers: One Hundred Clever Things We Take For Granted Which Have Changed Our Lives In The Last One Hundred Years* (Seven Dials/Cassell, 1998), reprinted by permission of the publisher; **Unit 17**: from Barry Miles, *Paul McCartney: Many Years From Now* (Vintage Books, 1998), © Barry Miles, 1997, reprinted by permission of The Random House Group Ltd; **Unit 19**: from A.A. Milne, *Winnie the Pooh* (Methuen, 1926), reprinted by permission of Egmont Books Ltd; **Unit 20**: 'Tennis serves up homes for mice' from *The Northern Echo* (25 June 2001), reprinted by permission of the publisher; **Unit 21**: Sarah Getty, 'Dragon attacks star's husband' from *Metro*, Newcastle, reprinted by permission of the publisher; **Unit 22**: from Ernest Hemingway, *To Have and Have Not* (Penguin Books, 1937), reprinted by permission of The Random House Group Ltd; **Unit 25**: 'To get the best from your video recorder' instructions from Philips Electronics UK Ltd; **Unit 26**: from Katharine Dart, 'Grubbing in the Dark' (BASF/*Daily Telegraph* Young Science Writer Awards, 2000); **Unit 27**: from '5 simple steps to take action', adapted from a Greenpeace promotional leaflet, reprinted by permission of Greenpeace UK; **Unit 28**: 'Race wars: are our schools to blame?' from *The Week* (21 July 2001), reprinted by permission of the publisher; **Unit 30**: book review by Chris Cross of *The Black Dogs of Doom* by Anthony Masters (Bloomsbury Publishing, 2001), reprinted by permission of Chris Cross.

Every effort has been made to trace or contact all copyright holders. The publishers would be pleased to rectify any omissions brought to their notice at the earliest opportunity.

Photographic credits

Unit 13: *Rum: Nature's Island* cover photograph: Lorne Gill (Courtesy: Scottish Natural Heritage); **Unit 15**: The Cholmondeley Ladies, © Tate, London 2001 (Courtesy: Tate Enterprises); **Unit 16**: Fish fingers packaging (Courtesy: Birds Eye Wall's); **Unit 17**: *Paul McCartney: Many Years From Now* cover photograph: Don McCullin (Courtesy: Abner Stein); **Unit 20**: 'Tim' the harvest mouse in Bristol photograph: David Jones/PA (Courtesy: PA Photos); **Unit 24**: India: Taj Mahal (Courtesy: Global Scenes/Indian Tourist Board); **Unit 28**: Bradford racial conflict photograph: Owen Humphreys (Courtesy: PA Photos); **Unit 29**: Pieman and costers; unnamed artist, from an engraving in Henry Mayhew's *London Labour and the London Poor* (Courtesy: Mary Evans Picture Library); **Unit 30**: *The Black Dogs of Doom* cover photograph: Photonica; Cover design: Nathan Burton (Courtesy: Bloomsbury Publishing plc).

Illustrations by: **Tom Cross**, pages 48 and 52; **Linda Jeffrey**, pages 6, 12, 18, 30 and 38; **Carol Jonas**, pages 4, 14, 16, 26 and 54; **Ruth Palmer**, pages 8, 10, 20, 24 and 46.